HOW TO WRITE A
BOOK
PROPOSAL

HOW TO WRITE A
BOOK
PROPOSAL

Michael Larsen

Writer's
Digest
Books

Cincinnati, Ohio

Some material from Michael Larsen's book on agents appears here in a slightly different form courtesy of Writer's Digest Books.

How to Write a Book Proposal. Copyright © 1985 by Michael Larsen. Printed and bound in the United States of America. All rights reserved. No part of this book may be reproduced in any form or by any electronic or mechanical means, including information storage and retrieval systems without permission in writing from the publisher, except by a reviewer, who may quote brief passages in a review. Published by Writer's Digest Books, an imprint of F&W Publications, Inc., 1507 Dana Avenue, Cincinnati, Ohio 45207. First paperback printing 1990.

Other fine Writer's Digest Books are available from your local bookstore or direct from the publisher.

96 95   7 6

Library of Congress Cataloging in Publication Data

Larsen, Michael.
   How to write a book proposal.

   Bibliography: p.
   Includes index.
   1. Book proposals. I.Title.
PN161.L37 1985   808'.02   85-3226
ISBN 0-89879-419-6

Acknowledgments

Although I accept full responsibility for this book's faults, I am grateful to be able to share with a multitude any praise for its virtues.

This book sprouted out of a book that Editor-in-Chief Carol Cartaino asked me to write. Writer's Digest wanted a book that would provide complete and honest answers to writers' endless questions about agents. It was courageous of her to look West instead of East for such a book, and I appreciate the faith that she, Budge Wallis, and Mert Ransdell had in me. I didn't realize that my attempt, in the course of this, to answer another oft-repeated plea—"How do I put together a Book Proposal?"—would end up between an entirely different set of covers.

It's been more than a decade since my partner Elizabeth and I sold our first nonfiction book on the basis of a proposal. Since then, we have learned about proposals from a great many people: clients, agents, and editors; the authors of the books in the bibliography; the instructors and the hundreds of writers we have spoken to at writing classes and conferences; and the students in the workshops I have given on how to prepare proposals. To all of them, my thanks.

For permission to quote from their proposals, I would like to thank the following writers: David Armstrong, Leon Fletcher, Phyllis Sheon Koppelman, Michael Lillyquist, Len Lyons, John Markoff, Chris Morgan, Arthur Naiman, William Paxson, Joanne Pugh, Lyn Reese, Michelle Saadi, Fred Setterberg, Randy Shilts, Lynda Van Devanter, and Jean Wilkinson. Special thanks go to Charles Rubin for allowing me to use his proposal in its entirety.

By providing me with a forum to teach workshops at the Media Alliance, Annette Dornbos and the membership of the Alliance also contributed to the creation of this book. In recognition of the fact that as the media go, so goes the country, and in appreciation of the opportunity the Alliance has given me as well as its efforts to make the media more open and responsible, I am contributing 10% of my income from the book to the Alliance.

I am grateful to rights specialist Barbara Zimmerman for checking the section on permissions.

For reading the book in various stages and for their advice and encouragement, I would like to single out the following editors: Michael Korda, Luther Nichols, Doris Ober, James Raimes, and John Thornton; these writers: William Paxson and Kary Schulman; and these agents: Marcia Amsterdam, Arthur Orrmont, Charlotte Sheedy, and Oscar Collier; and of course, my agent, Peter Skolnik.

I hope that every writer has the opportunity to work with an editor as conscientious as Beth Franks. I admit I didn't relish making all the changes that she, her colleague Howard Wells, and copyeditor Bill Betts suggested, but must also admit their recommendations improved the book greatly. So on your behalf as well as mine, I'd like to thank them. Thanks also to production editor Joan Bloss for marshaling the manuscript into book form.

Despite my problems with Valdocs 1.16, and a Comriter II printer that didn't work right for more than a year (a lust for revenge? Me?), this book would not have been written as quickly or rewritten as well, if I hadn't had an Epson QX-10. A computer encourages revision by making it easy to do, and the QX-10 makes it almost irresistible because it's so easy to use. What it does for the revision process alone makes a computer as valuable to a writer as a dictionary.

My lasting gratitude also goes to my family—my brother Ray and his wife Maryanne, my sister-in-law Carol Larsen, Rita Pomada, Alberta Cooper, and Sally Ross—for their valuable, continuing support.

I am lucky to have as my helpmeet my partner Elizabeth Pomada, who indeed helped me every step of the way, including reading the manuscript in more incarnations than she deserved to endure. Neither words nor royalties can repay her contribution to my work and my life. Actually, a little place overlooking the Mediterranean in Antibes might do, so if you hear about one, let me know.

For Elizabeth
who learned the hard way about the perils
of accepting a very short proposal
with no outline or sample chapter

CONTENTS

Introduction:
A Look Before You Leap

Book editors have an insatiable craving for new writers and new ideas. It is easier than ever to sell a well-conceived, well-written book that the American public will go into bookstores and buy. There are more publishers and more subjects to write about than ever.

The challenge is to get the right proposal to the right editor at the right publisher at the right time.

There is no uniform standard for a book proposal. Agents and editors vary in what they want to see. My approach to preparing a proposal has evolved through trial and error since my partner, Elizabeth Pomada, and I started our literary agency in 1972. Since then, we have sold books to more than 60 publishers.

The recommendations in this book provide a definite, specific method for preparing a proposal that is flexible enough to encompass the wide range of nonfiction subjects, as well as the varying approaches to writing about them and publishing them. For example, a book about business can be an exposé, a biography, a serious study, a humor book, a how-to, a series of interviews, or a heavily illustrated book. The book can be published as a mass market or trade paperback, or a hard cover book.

How to Write a Book Proposal presents not *the* way to write a proposal, but *one* way, a way that works for our writers and the editors we sell to. This book is not a substitute for trusting your instincts and using your common sense. If something works better for you than what you find here, we'd like to know about it to make the next edition of the book better. Please send us suggestions based on your adventures in Proposal Land. *Bon Voyage!*

How to Get the Most Out of This Material

The following four Rs will help you make the most effective use of *How to Write a Book Proposal*:
1. *Read it* through thoroughly.
2. *Refer to it* as you write your proposal.
3. *Reach out.* Join or start a writers' group. This will enable you to learn

from responses to your proposal as you write it. (The most helpful group will include writers with more experience. A group of beginners can provide support but not too much in the way of guidance.)

4. *Reread the instructions* once you've finished writing your proposal to make sure you've included everything about the book and about yourself that a publisher needs to know. While you should adapt this book's guidelines to suit your book, avoid adding things to your proposal which aren't called for.

CHAPTER ONE

The Challenge

How would you like $1,000,000 to write a book? The subject? You can pick one later. Does this sound like a fantasy? It happened to Bob Woodward. The catch is that it happened after his fourth book in a row hit the top of the best-seller list.

But here you sit with an exciting idea for a nonfiction book. Maybe it's a cookbook, or the story of an important yet unheralded artist whose life cries out for a biography, or a fast-breaking news story that has riveted the country's attention, or a revolutionary new technique for improving one's health, or a new solution to a social problem.

Whatever it is, your book demands to be written. Readers will love it, and it will earn you a hefty income and a solid reputation. Writing the book may be the greatest challenge of your life, but you're ready for it.

Yet you hesitate because you need money to do the book, you're not sure there'll be an audience for the book, or it's about somebody in to-day's headlines and you're worried that another book will beat yours to the bookstores. So before you spend six months, a year, or perhaps even longer on the project, you want a commitment for its publication and an advance against royalties to write it.

Perhaps one day book buyers will be so anxious to read your books that you too will command million-dollar advances. Until that happy day arrives, you have two ways to sell your nonfiction book: with a proposal or with a complete manuscript.

Even though editors will request revisions, when they start out with a complete manuscript, they know what they've got. With a proposal, an editor's enthusiasm is tempered with concern about whether you can and will finish the manuscript, whether you will complete it on time, and how well it will turn out.

To prove that a writer can sustain plot and characterization for at least 200 pages, or 50,000 words, and to create maximum impact on an editor, first novels usually have to be finished. Nonfiction writers are luckier, however. Since most nonfiction books rely on an accumulation of infor-mation rather than dramatic force to be effective, and since writers usu-ally need money to research and write their books, most nonfiction books are sold on the basis of proposals.

What is a Proposal?

Although it can be shorter or longer, a proposal generally ranges from 35 to 70 pages. It has two primary functions:

1. It's a selling tool.

The fundamental goal of a proposal is to use as few words as possible to generate as much enthusiasm as possible for your book from your idea, your style, your project's commercial potential, your ability to promote it, or ideally all four.

2. It's a writing tool.

Regard it as a long letter, memo, or report in which you are outlining for an editor and yourself what you are planning to do and why.

Even if you already have a complete manuscript, three other reasons justify submitting a proposal rather than the whole book:

First, the editor and the other people in the publishing house who must approve the project will get to and through a small pile of pages faster than a large pile.

Second, one of the creative satisfactions in an editor's life is helping to shape an idea into its most effective form. Shaping a book is much easier if it hasn't been written yet. You and your book will benefit from the opportunity to develop your project to suit an editor and a house.

Third, the promise of something is often more intriguing than the ultimate reality. An editor may envision a better book than you have written. And while you should indicate how much of your manuscript is finished, if editors only see a proposal, they may suggest how to improve the manuscript before they see it.

What will convince a cautious editor to take the plunge on your proposal? When you buy any product or service, you're buying the benefit it provides. A book basically has one of two benefits: information or entertainment. When you bought your copy of *The Elements of Style*, you bought it for its wisdom about writing. You bought it to help you become a better writer. That's the benefit it provides. That it is also entertaining and an exquisite example of the virtues it advocates is a bonus.

An adman once said that every line of advertising copy must accomplish two things:

1. Sell the product.

2. Sell the next line of copy.

Your proposal must sell your idea, your book, yourself, and the next line of copy. It should contain every morsel of information about the project and yourself, proving that the benefit you want to deliver is worth financing and that you possess the skill and experience necessary to deliver the finished manuscript.

A Working Marriage

Writing and publishing a book involve a series of working marriages between the writer and an idea, a collaborator perhaps, an agent, an editor, and a publishing house.

Preparing a proposal allows you the chance to prove to yourself that you really want to do the book and will enjoy working on it. The time you spend writing your proposal is a trial marriage between you and the idea. If you are going to have a problem with the project, it is far better to discover it before you are committed to writing the book.

Nine Criteria for a Salable Idea

The French President Georges Pompidou once remarked: "Conception is much more fun than delivery." But a poorly conceived book leaves itself open to responses like the one Samuel Johnson sent to an aspiring writer: "Your manuscript is both good and original; but the part that is good is not original, and the part that is original is not good."

The ideal idea is both good and original. Since your proposal flies or dies with your idea, that's the place to begin. Philip Roth once observed: "Nothing bad can happen to a writer. Everything is material." Everything you know, everything you do, and everything you are may lead to an idea for a book or find its way into your books. Ideas can come from conversation, your imagination, the media. They can even come from subjects you are knowledgeable, passionate, or curious about, or need to know more about.

One of my favorite *New Yorker* cartoons shows two women nursing cocktails in a posh restaurant, one happily announcing to the other: "I'm marrying Marvin. I think there's a book in it." As if agreeing with her, William Sloane states in *The Craft of Writing*: "There are no uninteresting subjects, only uninteresting writers."

The ability to come up with salable book ideas is a gift. Ideas themselves are gifts. And if you can't believe that God is whispering them in your ear, regard them as missives from one part of yourself to another.

Challenging ideas present you with the opportunity to grow as a person and a writer. The closer you come to realizing your ideas, the more they will change you, advancing your quest to reach your greatest potential as a writer and a human being.

The idea for your book should correspond to your interests and abilities. Before pushing ahead with it, evaluate your idea by asking yourself these questions:

1. Is my idea original?

Does it involve an unheralded figure, a new concept or endeavor, a relatively unexplored setting or historical period?

If you've hit upon an idea that is truly original and seems wildly commercial, consider these two possibilities: Either you have created a great opportunity for yourself or there's a good reason why the book hasn't already been done.

My partner Elizabeth and I were having a drink with an editor, and somehow the conversation led to the realization that no book existed on the cultural history of Greenwich Village. We were both turned on by the idea, since we had both spent time in the Village and remained captivated by its mystique. I convinced Elizabeth that she would enjoy researching the book and meeting the artists and writers who had lived there.

She planned a short illustrated book, but she took five years to finish it because she had to research seven books to write one: the history of art, poetry, theater, movies, music, dance, and the Village itself. As Elizabeth's bibliography will prove, there was a damn good reason why no one had ever written *America's Left Bank*, but unfortunately, Elizabeth didn't figure out what it was until after her agent had gotten her a contract for it!

2. If my idea isn't original, does it present a fresh slant on an old idea?

Your book must fill a hole either in the marketplace or on a publisher's list. Unless a subject is hot, publishers generally try to avoid duplication. They may still be interested, however, if they think there's enough room in the marketplace for similar books on a subject and feel that their houses wield the marketing muscle to make those books successful.

If you want to write about a subject that's already been covered, find a way to give the material the right spin, a new angle or approach for delivering the benefit of information or entertainment that will entice readers to buy the book.

Two books published by J. P. Tarcher created an immediate impact when they were published around the turn of the decade and have enjoyed continuing sales: Betty Edwards's *Drawing on the Right Side of the Brain* and Marilyn Ferguson's *The Aquarian Conspiracy: Personal and Social Transformation in the 1980s*. Both presented a new perspective on old subjects—how to be creative and how to change society—and both struck a responsive chord with readers.

3. Is it a subject I want to know more about?

This may not be important if it's a book you feel you can churn out quickly without any particularly positive feelings (not a state of mind conducive to producing your best or most salable work). But writing a book can be an emotional disaster if you wind up hating what you're writing about, a quandary biographers especially should try to resolve before they start to relive their subject's life. On the other hand, if you have an unquenchable thirst for knowledge about a subject or you're already bursting with information about it, you might be aching to get started.

4. How many people will be interested in my idea?

If you expect your book to be a hard cover, do you think enough book buyers will part with 15 bucks or more for it two years from now to make it worth a publisher's investing in the project?

Standards vary for how many copies a book has to sell to make it worth publishing. For a small publisher or a high-priced book, 3,000 copies might be enough. Large houses sooner or later want their books to achieve five-figure sales. One editor I know wants the books she buys to warrant 50,000-copy first printings.

During one of my proposal workshops, Fred Setterberg prepared a proposal for a book called *Up the Nonprofit Organization: A Survival Guide to Nonprofit, Community, and Volunteer Organizations.* The proposal was praised but turned down by more than 20 publishers.

Then Fred's coauthor Kary Schulman came up with the bright idea of presenting the same information but changing the subtitle and the slant of the book to *How You Can Succeed in Your Nonprofit, Community, and Volunteer Group.* We submitted the revised proposal to three publishers, and one of them, a major house at which two editors had previously turned the project down, paid a handsome advance for it. Why? Because the authors had broadened the market for the book from just organizations to the millions of Americans who work in volunteer groups. Ironically, the final title is *Beyond Profit: The Complete Guide to Managing the Nonprofit Organization.*

Another way to enlarge the potential audience for your book is for the idea to combine two salable areas of interest such as computers and law, business and medicine, or fitness and cooking.

You must first convince yourself that book buyers across the country will want to read your book, then convince the publisher.

5. Does my idea have enough depth for a book?

The amount of time and space a person or event receives in the media isn't necessarily an indication of a subject's depth, the longevity of its appeal, or its potential as a book. Most of what is news today won't be news tomorrow.

At the same time, if you come across your idea in a magazine or newspaper, speed may be vital—it's foolish to suppose that in our global village you are ever alone with an idea. Ideas are in the air because the raw material for them is in the people, events, and media which create and sustain the zeitgeist, the spirit, passions, and interests of the moment. If an idea is worth pursuing, follow up on it as quickly as you can without sacrificing quality.

Examining a story objectively as it evolves to gauge whether it has enough scope and whether the characters involved are intriguing enough to sustain a book; asking writers, readers, and booksellers about the idea; reading books which originated as news stories; and doing the research required to write your proposal will convince you whether or not your idea will yield a book's worth of information that will interest a national audience.

6. Will my book stand the test of time, or will it be here today and gone tomorrow?

Publishers are extremely sensitive to a subject's moment in time. They like to jump on bandwagons but not too early or too late, and the bandwagon can hold only so many players. When too many of them jump on at the same time, the result is "bookicide": too many houses pounce on a topic, flood the bookstores with "book-alikes," and quickly satiate book-buyer interest in the topic. Just because you see books in stores now on the subject you want to write about doesn't mean there will be interest in your book by the time it lands on the shelves.

The Boom That Went Bust

In the rush to get books on the shelves during the throes of the recent computer-book boom, writers turned in manuscripts on specific machines but by the time they finished them, either the machines bombed, the companies that made them went out of business, or publishers cut back on their lists because of the glut of introductory me-too books. The writers had wasted their time writing the books and didn't get the rest of their advances because the publishers wouldn't pay for books they had no hope of selling.

Check the mix of books on the best-seller list. It hasn't changed in decades: biography, history, current affairs, trends, humor, religion, business, reference, and the ever popular self-help books for body, mind, and spirit and for work, home, and leisure. These areas reflect continuing interests of the book-buying public and remain strong areas for salable new ideas. Despite the shakeout in computer books, technology, along with science and futurism, is a strong area.

It's been said that the difference between a fad and a trend is that a trend has an underlying economic basis. CB radio, disco dancing, and Rubik's cube created waves of excitement and books. Then the tide receded, leaving unsold books high and dry on booksellers' shelves.

If your idea is about a trend, read John Naisbitt's *Megatrends* (a 1984 Warner paperback) to see if it's in tune with where the country is heading. You could spend the rest of your career writing about the ideas in *Megatrends*. It's a gold mine of book ideas.

New York's publishing world is small; editors often know through the grapevine what's in the works at other houses. Once one publisher signs up a book on a subject, especially a hot topic, it may be harder to place another, even if it promises to be better.

7. Do I have the right focus for the book?

Finding the right focus for your book is essential. As one wag put it: "You shouldn't start vast projects with half-vast ideas." However, if the scope of your project is too broad, the book may be too difficult to do or too diffuse in its appeal to have a strong impact. It's the difference between the scattershot effect of a shotgun and using a rifle to draw a bead on your subject. For example, general books on sports don't do as well as books on specific sports.

On the other hand, if your idea is too narrow, it won't interest enough of the public that publishers must reach. A book about trumpeter Miles Davis's bebop years in Harlem will only appeal to music scholars and the most avid fans; a full-scale biography will be of interest to anyone who wants to understand modern jazz.

8. Will the book have enough commercial potential for both me and a publisher?

The idea for your book sets in motion a long process. Preparing your proposal, selling it, writing the book, and seeing it through publication with a large publisher usually takes a year and a half to two years. Your idea must have enough intrinsic interest and commercial appeal, for you as well as the publisher, to survive that time.

If you want to write the book for love, and you don't care how much money it makes, that's your choice, but remember that even if you're not fussy about lucre, publishers are. Their financial goal is simple: Make as much as possible out of the budget they have to invest in new books.

With the costs of editing, designing and producing the camera-ready mechanical, manufacturing, selling the book and its subsidiary rights, warehousing, shipping, promoting, and doing the accounting for a book, and a publisher's general expenses such as rent, utilities, and administration which are apportioned among all of its books, the average investment a major publisher makes in a book is more than $40,000 and rising. To this investment must be added the varying costs of the author's advance and printing the books. Small publishers have smaller overheads, pay smaller advances, and have to sell fewer copies of a book to break even, but with expenses like these to contend with, every publisher wants every book to pull its own weight.

9. Will my idea help me achieve my literary goals?
To become what you want to be as a writer, you must establish literary goals for yourself and evaluate a project taking both the short view—will you enjoy doing it and will it pay the rent—and the long view—will it help get you where you want to go as a writer? If you are serious about developing your career as a writer, motivate yourself with literary goals that both enable you to make a living and generate your best efforts.

Ultimately, as in all things, you must trust your instincts about risking your time, effort, and reputation. But you shouldn't go wrong if you choose a subject you can write about with pride and passion, and write the book you would buy if you wanted the information it contains. The more your book helps readers to reach their personal or professional goals, the more it will help you reach yours.

HOT TIP *As a writer, your capital is your time, your ideas, and your ability to turn them into salable material. Keep a notebook or tape recorder handy so you can make a note of ideas whenever they hit you. Keep an idea file for future reference and don't limit yourself to book ideas. Sooner or later, you may find a use for anything that you think is worth noting. Those minutes when you're drifting between being asleep and awake can bring unexpected insights, so be prepared.*

Examine your ideas with an eye to recycling them in as many media as possible. Books, software, data bases, video and audio cassettes, movies, television, and articles (which, over time, can be rewritten and resold to American and foreign trade and consumer newspapers and magazines) are all potential outlets for your work. Choose the right subject area and you may be able to carve a career out of it.

The Strongest Link

The biggest book chain in the world is not Waldenbooks or B. Dalton; it's the invisible chain linking ideas with readers. Depending upon their receptivity, competence, and persistence, everyone who comes between your idea and your readers—you, your agent, your editor and publisher, reviewers, librarians, and booksellers—is either a barrier or a conduit in communicating your idea.

As the first and most important link in the chain, consider yourself as being in the service of your idea. Be prepared to surrender every iota of energy, passion, imagination, integrity, and perseverance you can muster to the goal of creating the best book you are capable of. Strive to make your contribution to communicating your idea a source of excitement and inspiration to the next link in the chain. Your contribution begins with your proposal.

Checking the Competition

When you think you have a salable idea, your first task is to research other books written on the subject. Talk to librarians and booksellers about your idea. They're on the front lines and know firsthand what people are reading. They may be able to save you wasted effort or steer you in the right direction.

Ask if other books on the subject have been best-sellers. Find out if they were published by large publishers who because of their overheads have larger expectations for their books than small publishers. How well similar books have done may indicate how yours will fare.

Two of the joys of the literary life are browsing in libraries and bookstores and buying books. Become friends with the booksellers in your area who love books. Buying books and discussing your favorites is all you have to do. Like book lovers in general, booksellers thrive on their passion for good books, and they light up when they find a kindred soul with whom they can share their latest discovery. Someday, they will be stocking your book and might even throw an autographing party for you.

HOT TIP *Asking booksellers and librarians about books they have requests for that they can't fulfill is an excellent way to find a need and fill it. Also check with experts in the field about books they want but can't find.*

If booksellers resist your idea, find out why and if you agree with them, change the focus of your book to overcome their resistance. If you can't, you may be in trouble because the sales representatives who service them are already aware of their feelings, and editors reject books their reps can't sell. If you have an idea that belongs between covers, you should be able to garner support for it from knowledgeable, trustworthy members of your local book community.

Read All About It

If booksellers are receptive to your idea, read all competitive books on the subject, including those mentioned in bibliographies. To track down competitive books at libraries and bookstores, check these five sources:

1. *Books in Print (BIP)*, an annual published in ten volumes which lists every book in print in the United States by title, author, and subject. Book distribution is so uneven that if local bookstores or libraries don't have a book on the subject you're researching, it may still be elsewhere, which is why the subject guide in *BIP* is the most reliable source to what's available.

2. *Forthcoming Books*, issued bimonthly, lists the books announced since the latest edition of *BIP*.

3. *Publishers Weekly*, the weekly trade journal, puts out huge spring and fall announcement issues in which publishers advertise their upcoming titles.

4. *Publishers Weekly Yearbook: News, Analyses, & Trends in the Book Industry* is a handy illustrated compendium of lists, statistics, and articles about what happened in trade publishing the previous year.

5. *Publisher's Trade List Annual (PTLA)* lists books by publisher so you can see which publishers are most interested in your subject. Writing for the catalogs of those publishers will enable you to get a better feel for the character of different publishers.

For virtually any kind of book you want to write, models—both bombs and best-sellers—abound. Reading comparable books will help you to:
- offer something different and better
- anticipate the standards of form and content expected of books on the subject
- judge how your work measures up
- glean information you need to describe the competition to editors
- develop a list of potential publishers

Books not in local bookstores or libraries are often available through interlibrary loans.

Reading between the lines to discern what hasn't been covered or covered thoroughly may help you refine your idea and plant the seeds for other book ideas. Underlining or taking notes about the book's strengths and weaknesses will enable you to reassure an editor about competitive books in your proposal.

Also read books which will complement yours. Best-selling books on a subject which won't compete with your book help sell it by proving there's a market for books on the subject. The publishers of these books may buy yours. If, for instance, you wanted to write a biography of comedian Dan Aykroyd, the success of Bob Woodward's best-seller *Wired*, the story of Aykroyd's *Saturday Night Live* colleague John Belushi, might help prove the commerciality of the project.

Test-Marketing Your Idea

Getting an article about the subject published is an excellent method for test-marketing your idea. Researching the article will help you determine whether there's a book in the subject. Writing it will give you a feeling for how well you handle the subject, the problems involved in writing the book, how long it will take, and how much you will enjoy writing it. The experience will help you decide if you are a sprinter (article writer) or a marathoner able to go the distance.

If you need to interview hard-to-get people for the book, they will be more likely to agree to talk if you're on assignment for a magazine than if you're just doing research for an unsold proposal.

In both a literary and a commercial sense, an article can be the embryo from which your book evolves. The periodical you sell the article to, the price you get for it, and the reaction from editors and readers are valuable gauges of the book's appeal. Responses from readers may correct mistakes and provide new facts, sources, and lines of inquiry.

One or more articles that are long enough and strong enough can function as sample material. An article may even sell the book. Agents and editors read magazines and newspapers trying to unearth writers and ideas. If an outstanding article catches the right person's fancy, you may not even need to write a proposal, or only a brief one.

The Downside

An article does involve risk because another writer may also decide to do a book on the subject. To lessen this danger and stimulate responses from readers, agents, and editors, ask the editor of the publication to state on the first page of the article that it is from a book in progress. This suggests that you have a head start and may deter potential competitors while attracting buyers.

Since your proposal may not sell, placing an article will help offset the cost of your research. If the article is popular enough, it may lead to additional articles on the subject, which will aid your research and increase the chances of selling the idea as a book.

Keep in mind, though, that magazines may offer less for an article than they would for first-serial rights—pre-publication extracts from your book. The best time for an article based on your book to appear is when books are in the stores so that if readers like the article, they will go buy the book. Selling articles long before publication will lessen a publisher's ability to sell the book and may hinder first-serial sales when the time comes. This is particularly true with books containing earth-shaking revelations. You can only let the cat out of the bag once.

However, if you need the money or the potential help in selling the proposal, don't hesitate.

HOT TIP   *First-time authors may find the prospect of writing a book less intimidating if they look at it as a series of long articles.*

The Parts of a Proposal

Some writers find it easier to write a book than a proposal. For others, writing the proposal is the most creative, pleasurable aspect of doing a book. You have the freedom to brainstorm and plan the book in the form that pleases you without the responsibility for writing it and the pressure of a deadline that goes along with a contract.

Although there is no one way to write a proposal any more than there is to write a book, we have found this approach effective with editors.

A proposal has three parts in a logical sequence, each with a specific goal. An editor must be sufficiently impressed with each part of the proposal to go on to the next.

The Introduction

The goal of the Introduction is to prove that you have a solid, marketable, practical idea and that you are a pro. The Introduction usually has three parts: an *Overview*, *Resources Needed to Complete the Book*, and *About the Author*.

The Chapter-by-Chapter Outline

A paragraph to a page of prose outlining every chapter proves that you have thought the project through, that there's a book's worth of material in the idea, and that you have devised the best structure to organize it.

Sample Chapters

One or more sample chapters, depending on the nature of the book, shows you and an editor how the outline will grow into a manuscript and how well you can write about the subject.

In addition to how commercial the idea is and how well your style fits the subject, an editor will consider:

- your professional experience
- how much time and money the book will require
- whether you've chosen a suitable structure for the book
- impressive samples of your published work
- how the proposal looks

Piles to Go Before They Sleep

Keep in mind what editors' lives are like. During office hours, they're busy with meetings and phone calls, so, like agents, they spend their nights and weekends wading through ream after ream of proposals and manuscripts, and also like agents, rejecting more than 90 percent of them in the perpetual hunt for projects they like and out of which their houses can wring a profit. The hardest part of the job for most editors, and agents, is finding salable books, but that's what their jobs depend on.

Your proposal will be in competition with every idea, proposal, manuscript, and book that an overworked, underpaid editor has ever read, bought, rejected, and heard about. That's thousands of books, and the number keeps growing.

You can't expect editors to take the time to tutor you on how to improve your grammar or your proposal. If your idea, your style, or the way you've put your proposal together isn't as strong as it has to be, if you give editors *any* reason to say no, they will, and move on quickly to the next project in the bottomless pile. Many editors use assistants to screen material for them. An assistant's report may seal the fate of a submission without the editor ever laying eyes on it.

Even if an editor likes your proposal, that's only the beginning. The editor usually has to convince an editorial board, which may include members of the editorial, sales, publicity, production, and subsidiary rights departments, and company officers. Your proposal should not supply them with ammunition to shoot the project down.

Appealing to the Big Apple

If you want your proposal to appeal to New York editors, write with a perspective that will impress them. Their tastes and interests may be catholic, and their sensibilities sophisticated, but they (rightly) regard themselves as living in the capital of the world. Although as a group, editors are liberal, sensitive, and caring people, they are victims of an urban yet provincial mentality. If a trend hasn't been officially sanctioned by its appearance in *Newsweek, The Wall Street Journal,* or *The New York Times,* it doesn't exist.

One of our writers once suggested that the criminal justice establishment requires perpetually rising crime rates to justify its existence and its cost. He felt that crime rates weren't as bad as the statistics indicated. Although this may be true for the country as a whole, telling that to New York editors who live in fear of being mugged or burglarized was asking for trouble!

If your book will have a conservative political slant, it may offend editors' liberal sensibilities, so take this into consideration in presenting your idea.

To keep up with news about writing and publishing, subscribe to *Writer's Digest, The Writer, Publishers Weekly,* and *The New York Times Book Review.* If you are really determined to keep in touch with the editorial environment, the editorial mindset, subscribe to *Newsweek* and *The New York Times.*

Why What's First May Be Last

The seventeenth-century philosopher Blaise Pascal once observed: "The last thing we find in making a book is to know what we must put first." Not until you have finished researching your proposal and assembled all the material you want to include will you be able to provide all the information the proposal needs, including the strongest opening.

These instructions are presented in the order that the editor will read the proposal, not in the order that you will research and write it. While avoiding repetition, you will want to integrate the information in the three parts of the proposal. For instance, the Overview includes the number of pages that you plan to have in the finished manuscript. But you won't know that figure until you have written the Chapter-by-Chapter Outline.

Write your proposal in whatever order feels most comfortable. Once you have finished a draft of the whole proposal, you will see the gaps that have to be filled in and you can polish each part until it is complete and complements the rest of the proposal.

Now let's go step by step through the process of creating a proposal that will get you the contract and advance you need to write your book.

CHAPTER TWO

The Introduction

The Introduction of your proposal sets the standard for the tone, style, and quality of what follows. If you can't grab an editor with your Introduction, it's all over. Though they may be shorter or longer, most of the successful introductions we've seen run between five and ten pages. As mentioned earlier, the Introduction has three parts: the Overview, Resources Needed to Complete the Book, and About the Author.

The Overview

In the Overview, the challenge is to intrigue an editor with the essence of the book and make a case for its existence. To prove that you have a salable book idea, the Overview covers the following 13 topics:

1. The subject hook, creating interest in the subject, and the book hook, consisting of 2, 3, and 4 below
2. The title and subtitle
3. The book's selling handle
4. The length of the book
5. The book's other special features
6. The identification of a well-known authority who has agreed to write an introduction to the book (optional)
7. A sentence about what you have done to prevent technical and legal problems
8. Back matter
9. Markets for the book
10. Subsidiary rights
11. Spin-offs
12. What you will do to help promote the book
13. A list of books that will compete with and complement yours

Let's go over each of these elements and see how they can help make the case for your book.

1. The Subject Hook

When you go into a bookstore and start reading a book, how many pages do you give it before you either decide to put it back or buy it? Students in my workshops usually agree that one page is all they need to make a decision. If the book is interesting enough that they want to turn to page two, they'll buy the book. If not, they'll keep browsing.

Because page one shows why editors and book buyers will be interested in the subject and tells in a nutshell what the book will be, it is the most important page of the proposal. You must hook the editor to the subject and the book.

Start about four inches down the page and type:

Introduction

Overview

Then in the first paragraph or two of your Introduction, hook the editor to the subject with a quote, an event, an idea, or a joke. A subject hook can also be a compelling anecdote or statistic that rivets the editor's attention, or it can be both: an anecdote that gives rise to the statistic.

Assuming editors know only as much about the subject as the average reader, you must convince them that the subject warrants a book. For a journalist, it's like the lead paragraph in a newspaper or magazine story. At United Press International, the approach to writing a story is based on the belief that if you hook readers with the first six words, they will read the first paragraph. If they read the first paragraph, they will read the first three paragraphs, and if they stay with the story through the first three paragraphs, they'll finish it.

Here is an excellent example of hooking a reader from the beginning of Michelle Saadi's 56-page proposal for *Claiming Your Share: How to Get Full Payment and Protect Your Rights After an Auto Accident:*

After driving for 25 years without a single accident, John Smith had his car rear-ended as he stopped for a red light. He suffered neck and back injuries and lost two months of work. Instead of paying Mr. Smith, the other driver's insurance company went to court, convinced the jury Smith had made a panic stop, and won the case. Although he lost $5,000 and was an innocent victim, Smith never recovered a cent from the accident.

According to figures from the National Safety Council and the Insurance Information Institute, John Smith represents the one out of every five drivers who have accidents each year. There are 149 million drivers in this country and every year, they have 18 million accidents. Although most of these drivers carry insurance, many of the victims in these accidents, like Mr. Smith, recover nothing at all.

HOT TIP *Anecdotes are word pictures that can be worth a thousand words. They humanize a book by presenting a slice of life which readers have experienced or can empathize with, and which make for more enjoyable and memorable reading than just abstract ideas.*

People like to read about other people. That's why anecdotes are an effective way to get your points across. Make them read like little short stories that pack a wallop by being as humorous or dramatic or startling as possible. This is especially important for an anecdote which opens the proposal. An anecdote may take longer than a paragraph to tell. It may even require a page or more. But remember that the longer it is, the stronger it should be.

A statistic alone may suffice if it suggests a large potential market for the book. For instance, if you are going to write a book about a new method to stop smoking, the statistics on how many people smoke and the toll it takes in lives, health costs, and lost work time will convince an editor, who is aware of the problem in a general way, that the subject is worth another book.

Using round numbers and naming a reliable source lend credibility to your statement and to you as an authority on the subject. Dates, geography, money, size, the number of people, the growth of a trend—use whatever data will put the subject into context for an editor and prove that there is interest in the subject.

After you hook editors to the subject, hook them to the book with a two-sentence paragraph containing three pieces of information. In the first sentence, give the title, subtitle if you have one, and the selling handle for your book. In the second sentence, indicate the number of pages and illustrations the manuscript will have. I call this the book hook.

2. The Title and Subtitle

When I worked at Bantam, there was a story going around that the company once had high hopes for a book called *Five Days*, but it wasn't selling so they changed the name to *Five Nights* and it sold like hotcakes. The story isn't true but there's truth in it.

At one of his Writer's Digest writing seminars, Arky Gonzalez described the results of research to determine what article titles on a magazine cover would sell the most copies of the magazine. The two winners: "Proof Found of Personal Immortality" and "Pope's Daughter Found Murdered in Commie Love Nest."

What's in a name? Plenty! A provocative, selling title will definitely help put your book across with editors and book buyers. A symbol or metaphor that captures the essence of the book can crystallize the meaning and the structure of the book for you, the editor, and the reader.

Roots, for example, is a wonderfully evocative title which also helped Doubleday's art director choose the typeface and color for the jacket.

Passages is another simple, clear image, which was fortunate enough to be enhanced with Milton Glaser's beautiful artwork. (Paperback houses usually change cover art because a mass-market book, an impulse item which must grab the attention of browsers, needs harder-selling art than a hardcover book. But Glaser's rainbow of ascending steps is so effective that Bantam used it for the paperback edition.)

If you can sum up your book with just a title, so much the better. One of our books, Karen Lustgarten's *The Complete Guide to Disco Dancing*, didn't need a subtitle to become a best-seller. Other more recent books of ours are *How to Speak Like a Pro*, *Getting Started with the IBM PC and XT*, and *The Official Travis McGee Quiz Book*.

HOT TIP *When publishing people refer to a title, they only use one or two words, so do as they do: Keep it short and simple, six words or less, and add an explanatory subtitle if necessary. You will also help book buyers who are researching available books by subject if the first word of the title conveys the subject of the book.*

Alex Haley added the phrase *The Saga of an American Family*, which made it clear that *Roots* was a history told in chronological order. *Predictable Crises of Adult Life* was the subtitle Gail Sheehy chose to explain *Passages*.

These titles of our books combine an intriguing title and a subtitle that put across the benefit the book offers: *Advertising for Love: How to Play the Personals*; *Guerilla Marketing: Secrets for Making Big Profits from Small Businesses*; *Neptune's Apprentice: Adventures of a Commercial Fisherwoman*; *Bit by Bit: An Illustrated History of Computers*.

Don't get too far out or poetic with your title. Try it out on your network of book people and potential buyers of your book to see how they respond to it. Sacrifice imagery for clarity.

Remember that between the title and the subtitle, you must tell and sell: describe what the book is and motivate book buyers to pick it up off the shelf. Your title will get only one second of the casual browser's time. You must sell the sizzle as well as the steak. Try to make your title a big red flag that says: "Stop and look at me!"

Don't offer an editor a string of titles to choose from; pick one. And don't be overly concerned about finding the best title at this stage. The right title will help sell your project, but editors aren't buying your title, they're buying your book.

If you can't think of the best title, perhaps your agent or editor will, or you will as you are writing the book. Titles often change in the course of writing and producing a book. You will settle on whatever title you, your editor, and the sales department decide will give your book the best shot in a crowded marketplace.

When photographer Morley Baer and I were roaming around San Francisco shooting Victorian houses for a book we were collaborating on with my partner Elizabeth, he suggested that we call the book *Painted Ladies*. As soon as he said it, I laughed with delight and instant appreciation. It was the perfect title. We knew that we needed a subtitle and *San Francisco's _____ Victorians* was the logical choice, but we were stuck for the right adjective. Cy Nelson, our editor at Dutton, was right on target with the word *Resplendent*.

3. The Selling Handle

Michael Korda, the editor in chief at Simon & Schuster and a best-selling author himself, has a formula for a book's success: "If you can't describe a book in one or two pithy sentences that would make you or my mother want to read it, then of course you can't sell it."

San Francisco Bay Area sales rep Stan Gould once remarked in *Publishers Weekly*: "When we make our calls, we have on the average maybe 14 seconds per book [!]. . .what we need is an expeditious, concise, sales-oriented handle that says a lot about it in as few words as possible."

Your book passes through many hands on the road from writer to reader: agent, editor, salespeople, and booksellers. They all need a one-line handle to sell it to the next link in the publishing chain.

Broadway producer David Belasco's warning to playwrights also applies to you: "If you can't write your idea on the back of my calling card, you don't have a clear idea." The selling handle for your book will be a one-line statement of your goal for the book.

The handle may be its thematic or stylistic resemblance to an already successful book or author. Such comparisons are often used because they give booksellers an immediate grasp of a book. If you plan to write a French version of *Roots*, a book about financial "passages," or a book in the freewheeling style of Tom Wolfe, an editor will get the message.

Don't just think about what you're selling. Think about what readers are buying. Figure out what makes your book unique, what sets it off from the competition. Then create a concise, memorable phrase that conveys the book's content and appeal. You want to establish what in advertising is called your book's "marketing position." And since the best marketing position a product or service can have is to be the first of its kind, write—if it's true—that your book "will be the first book to . . ." (Since your book doesn't exist yet, always use the future tense when you refer to it.)

The selling handle should broadcast the benefit readers will gain from your book. If you have trouble coming up with a strong title or selling handle, try this: list the book's substance and benefits in the form of phrases. Then see if you can manipulate them to snare the essence of your book in an enticing phrase.

For *Where the Chips May Fall: The Peril and Promise of the Semiconductor Revolution*, John Markoff and Lenny Siegel wrote that it "will be the first book which documents the social, economic, and ethical consequences of the explosive growth of the 'miracle chip.' " (To illustrate how titles can change, the final title of this book was *The High Cost of High Tech: The Dark Side of the Chip*.)

In his 46-page proposal, Arthur Naiman called his book *Every Goy's Guide to Common Jewish Expressions*: "the first humorous yet accurate, concise yet comprehensive handy pocket dictionary of the 450 Jewish words that crop up most frequently in books, conversations, comedy routines, movies, and jokes."

In their 107-page proposal for *Home Before Morning: The Story of a Nurse in Vietnam*, Lynda Van Devanter and Christopher Morgan wrote that it would be "the first book to tell the story of a woman Vietnam veteran, the first book to shed light on this blind spot in our nation's vision."

Of his book *The Mayor of Castro Street: The Life and Times of Harvey Milk*, Randy Shilts wrote in his 79-page proposal that it "will chronicle the rise of both Milk and the gay movement he represented."

The handle in a 161-page proposal for an anthology edited by Lyn Reese, Jean Wilkinson, and Phyllis Sheon Koppelman called *I'm on My Way Running: Women Speak on Coming of Age* was: "a collection of writings in which women from different times and cultures reveal the joys and pains of coming of age."

Len Lyons wrote in his 34-page proposal: "*The 101 Best Jazz Albums: A History of Jazz on Records* will be the first jazz discography. It will serve both as a consumer's guide and a history of jazz told through discussions of the best available albums."

When he proposed *How to Speak Like a Pro*, Leon Fletcher wrote in his 91-page proposal that it "will present step-by-step, practical, platform-tested techniques and tips on how to plan and present effective speeches."

These handles vary in length, but as elsewhere in your proposal, the fewer words the better.

Editors resist what sounds self-serving. Let your idea, the facts supporting it, and your writing make your case. Unless you or your experience is part of the book, leave yourself out of it. Editors are wary of authors on ego trips. Write about the book, not about yourself.

Your proposal is a business document, not an opportunity to talk about yourself or about what you think you have in common with the editor. After you write the subject hook, unless you are the subject, write about your book.

However, if your knowledge or experience is the basis for the book, begin the book hook like this: "Based on the author's x years of experience as an x, (title) will be the first book to . . . ."

HOT TIP *Just as you should avoid the words "I," "we," "us," and "our" unless the book is about yourself, also avoid the word "you" in the Introduction and the Chapter-by-Chapter Outline. The first two parts of the proposal are directed to the editor, not the book buyer.*

If you want to address readers directly, as I am in this sentence, do it in the sample chapters.

---

4. The Length of the Book

It's been said that no good book is ever too long and no bad book ever too short. Growing production costs, however, are making editors increasingly receptive to shorter books.

The usual minimum length for a manuscript of straight text is 50,000 words or 200 pages. Humor books may be a fraction of that length, and biographies twice as long. Illustrated books may require less text.

The last part of the book hook is a sentence describing the book's length: "The finished manuscript will contain x pages and", if you plan to include illustrations, "x photographs, x drawings, x maps, and x charts." Editors assume illustrations are in black and white unless you indicate otherwise. Since illustrations will be on separate pages, don't count them as manuscript pages. (You will learn how to arrive at these numbers in the section on preparing an outline.)

Nonfiction manuscripts generally run between 200 and 400 typewritten double-spaced pages. Make your manuscript as long as it takes to do justice to the subject. But remember: The longer the manuscript, the higher the cover price, and prices affect sales. Publishers shy away from projects that will be too expensive to produce, resulting in higher list prices than they feel book buyers will tolerate.

HOT TIP   *When estimating the number of pages or, as you will in the next section of the Introduction, the number of months it will take to finish the manuscript, don't give a range such as 200 to 250 pages or six to nine months. Be specific and definite. Avoid the words* tentative, estimated, *or* approximately; *the editor knows you are guesstimating.*

Most of the time, finished manuscripts are not the length guessed at either in the proposal or in the contract. What is important is that you have a clear, decisive vision of your book.

I know a writer who wanted to do a how-to book about writing because he felt it would be a great help to writers. He had a four-page brochure he had been sending out with writing instructions, and with new information he had been gathering, he felt it would add up to 15 pages of manuscript, a good size for a little booklet.

But when he revised the material, he had 60 pages of manuscript. He began working with an editor who sent him editorial suggestions. He made them and then the manuscript was 87 pages. The editor then sent him nine single-spaced pages of corrections. Unhappy but persistent, he trudged on but then he found himself with a 137-page manuscript. And then came the copy editing. What was the final result of what started out to be a little booklet? You're holding it in your hands!

If you want your book to be a standard-size hard cover or mass-market or trade paperback, you don't have to mention format. If the book needs to be an unusual size, end this paragraph by indicating how you envision it. For example, if you are planning to use tax forms as illustrations, then an 8 ½" x 11" format might be better. But unless you feel that a large or unusual size is imperative, present it in a way that suggests you're flexible enough to change your mind if the publisher thinks another format will be more economical or salable. Large-format books are more expensive to produce and harder for booksellers to stock on small shelves.

One of the positive trends in the business is that publishers will produce a book in whatever format will sell the most copies and will recycle a title in other formats if they think it will sell.

Doing It by the Numbers

The value of providing an editor with specific numbers is threefold:

1. They give a sense of the book's size.
2. They show that you've thought the project through and convey the impression that you know what you're doing.
3. They help editors do their own proposals.

Successful projects usually have not one but three proposals behind them. First, the covering letter that accompanies the proposal which in effect is a proposal to an editor to read what follows. Then the proposal itself. And finally, a proposal-to-publish form which editors fill out when they want to buy a book.

This document, which may run six pages or longer, includes information about the book's content and virtues, the author, production costs, estimated sales, subsidiary rights potential, markets, promotion possibilities, and what it will cost the house to buy. The reactions of the editor's colleagues in the editorial, sales, promotion, production, and sub rights departments, fortified with a persuasive proposal-to-publish form, determine the fate of the project.

An editor will take your estimate of the manuscript's length to get a word count and use the number of words to figure out how many pages the book will run. This may range from 50 percent to 80 percent of your manuscript pages, depending on the size of the type and the space between the lines.

The page or trim size of the book also affects the number of words on the printed page. So don't be concerned about the number of pages your book will contain, just the number of 250-word typewritten pages you will write.

Once an editor knows the page length, he or she consults with the production department and obtains estimates of the unit cost, or manufacturing cost per copy, and the cover price—five to eight times the unit cost is one traditional yardstick. Your advance on royalties may be based on the estimated number of copies sold during the first year. Your royalty on each copy will be a percentage of either the cover price or the net price, which is what librarians and booksellers pay the publisher for it.

Then the editor subtracts part of the royalties as a reserve against booksellers' returns of unsold books and arrives at the advance to offer you for your book. A publisher will also consider the value of other sales such as classroom adoptions, foreign rights, paperback reprint, and book club sales. (More on these later.)

HOT TIP *If your book has the potential to be a series of books, it will make the project more valuable to a publisher. You may be on your way to a multibook contract, which will elevate the importance of you and the project to the house. If you want to propose the book as the first in a series, add a sentence to the book hook which reads: "(Title) will be the first in a series of x books including books on A, B, C, etc."*

Although a series of books is an attractive idea to publishers, it doesn't happen often. Suggest a series only if it's an integral part of the idea. An editor may hesitate to undertake a large project unless it promises to be a surefire hit. If the idea lends itself to other books, you can list them in the section on spin-offs.

5. The Book's Other Special Features

The next part of your Overview describes other important benefits the book will provide and also its tone. Will the book be humorous, serious, down-to-earth? What kind of personality will it have? What themes will it develop? Will it use anecdotes, checklists, chapter summaries, or exercises? If the nature of the illustrations the book will contain is not already clear, what will they be?

A biography is usually structured chronologically. A how-to book starts with the simplest elements of a skill and flows logically to the difficult aspects of it. If the book's structure isn't apparent from the nature of the project or how you explain it, tell the editor in a sentence how it will progress.

If you are proposing a picture book, describe your vision of the balance between text and illustrations.

If you are dividing the book into several parts, indicate in separate sentences what each will contain. Be brief to avoid repeating the outline.

6. An All-Star Introduction

If you can get a commitment for an introduction from someone whose name will add to the book's credibility and salability, mention who it is, his or her credentials if the person isn't well known, and how long the introduction will be—500 words will do. If you don't want to approach writers now, list the people you plan to contact for an introduction.

The two reasons to ask someone to do an introduction are equally important. The person's stature in the field should lend authority to the book, and the person's fame should convince browsers seeing the name on the jacket to pick the book up. Ask the person not to write anything until you finish the book, and don't pay for the introduction until your editor accepts it.

An editor may think an introduction isn't necessary or may have a better suggestion for a person to write it. Perhaps the editor can obtain an introduction from someone the house already publishes, which might save you money. If the person feels strongly enough about the project or you, he or she may do the project for the publicity and an autographed copy of your book. On the other hand, a well-known authority may ask for and deserve a dollar a word.

An M.D. or Ph.D. on the cover of a book about health, psychology, or another subject that requires an academic imprimatur assures an editor that you boast the right set of initials to tackle the idea. If you are invading a specialized field without being academically anointed, consider getting an intro from someone who does have credentials. In this case, the person doesn't have to be well known. Another solution to the problem is to collaborate with an expert.

7. Avoiding Technical and Legal Problems

If evaluating your proposal requires a particular expertise, an editor will have a specialist review it. Unless you have absolute confidence in the material, get your own expert to read it first. If you do, indicate who it is at this point.

Publishers are constantly hit with nuisance suits which cost them thousands of dollars a year, so they are extremely wary of books that may provoke litigation. If your research makes you aware of a possible legal problem because of libel, privacy, or copyright infringement, hire an experienced literary attorney to check the proposal and its supporting documents so you can assure an editor that a legal beagle has approved your proposal.

Literary attorneys are in short supply outside of New York, and though it is always better to work with someone you can meet with, experience is preferable to proximity. You can obtain the name of an attorney from national writers' and agents' organizations or through the following referral services:

Volunteer Lawyers for the Arts
36 West 44th Street
New York, NY 10036
(212) 575-1150

Bay Area Lawyers for the Arts
Room 255, Building C
Fort Mason, San Francisco, CA 94123
(415) 775-7200

Lawyers for the Creative Arts
111 North Wabash Avenue
Chicago, IL 60602
(312) 263-6989

Instant Query

Give your subject hook and your book hook the impact of a query letter. In fact, to test the waters before submitting your proposal, add the information from 5, 6, and 7, and a paragraph about yourself mentioning that you have an x-page proposal for the book, which can be completed in x months, and *voilà!*, you have a query letter ready to mail. If you've had an impressive article about the subject published, attach it to the letter. Multiple query letters to agents and editors are okay if you mention that it's a multiple query and try to avoid photocopies.

In addition to testing the waters, you may save yourself time and postage with a phone call or query letter before you submit your proposal. In responding to a query, an agent or editor might suggest a more salable slant for your book.

Another approach to testing the idea is to query after you do enough research to know that there's a book in the subject that you want to write but before you start the proposal. The trade-off here is the time lag between when an editor expresses interest and when the proposal is ready.

8. Back Matter

The last thing to mention about the contents of the book is what comes last: the back matter. List what you will include in the order it will appear: appendix, notes, glossary, bibliography, index. Without counting the index, end with the number of back-matter pages you will have. As with the rest of the proposal, being specific impresses editors. Librarians like bibliographies and indexes because they add to the book's value as a research tool. Publishers like to please librarians because school, college, and public libraries are among their largest customers.

Writers can usually list all back matter in one sentence. However, if you need a paragraph or more to describe your book's appendixes, use a separate page at the end of the outline to supplement your mention of them here.

HOT TIP *Avoid footnotes in your proposal. They are distracting and will make your proposal read like a term paper. If the book will have footnotes and you use them in the sample chapters, include them at the end of the proposal. Asterisks also interrupt the flow of the text. Avoid them except in the sample material.*

---

9. Markets for the Book

In the section on evaluating your idea, I mentioned the importance of proving the existence of the audience for your book to a publisher. Now's your chance. After you've discussed what your book will be, tell the editor in a sentence or a page or more who will buy it.

Ideally, your book will have four kinds of markets: people who will buy your book in book and specialty stores, long-term "back list" markets such as schools, and "special sales" markets. The more copies an editor thinks your book will sell, the more the editor will want it. So starting with the largest, describe the markets for your book:

Stores That Sell Books

The first market to cover is those parts of the American public who will go into a store and buy your book. Trade paperbacks and hardcover books are sold in the nation's 10,000 bookstores. Mass-market paperbacks are displayed on wire racks in 100,000 outlets such as drugstores, airports, and supermarkets.

You can present the book's readership with criteria such as age; sex; income; occupation, including professionals in your field; marital status; geography; education; religion or other beliefs; membership in organizations; interest in a sport, hobby, or other activity; statistics on sales of related books, magazines, or merchandise; the growing awareness of the subject because of television, films, advertising, or the news media; or attendance at events.

Use accurate figures that will verify that there's a large enough special-interest, regional, or national audience for your book to warrant publishing it. Be specific and factual, use round up-to-date numbers, and include sources to lend authority to your statements. Your librarian will point you to the best sources for the figures you need.

A statistic in your subject hook will give an editor a sense of the market for your book. For instance, in the subject hook quoted earlier for *Claiming Your Share*, Michelle Saadi mentions that there are 18 million accidents a year. This is how she amplified on that number in her section on markets:

"Since every driver in the United States averages one accident every five years, there will be a continuing market for this book. Part of this market will be 70 million female drivers, since *Claiming Your Share* will have three chapters discussing problems women face in getting fair settlements.

"A second potential market will be professional people whose work connects them with insurance claims. This group includes doctors, attorneys, private investigators, and the staffs of insurance companies.

"An additional market will be teachers who give classes and seminars on solving legal problems without an attorney."

Figures lend credibility and authority to your assertions, but you may not need them if the number of groups of potential readers you refer to is large enough or if there are obviously enough book buyers in the groups you mention to assure a market for your book. Here are two examples:

This is what William Paxson wrote about markets in his proposal for *Write It Now! A Time-Saving Guide to Writing Better Letters, Memos, Reports, and More:* "The market for this book consists of anyone who writes as part of the daily routine in business, government, and nonprofit organizations, or who is self-employed."

In her proposal for a cultural history of Greenwich Village in New York City, Elizabeth Pomada covered markets this way: "The markets for *America's Left Bank* will be both immediate and backlist: anyone who has ever lived in or dreamed of Greenwich Village, the 20 million visitors who spend $3 billion in New York every year, gift-givers, and college and high school classes studying cultural history."

Since editors are bandwagon jumpers, if there's a pattern of growth in the numbers you present, mention it. If, for instance, you want to write a book about videocassette recorders, the statistics on the growing number of consumers who are buying them will supply an editor with a powerful incentive to buy the book.

However, a circumstance in which numbers are not necessary is when you will be approaching an editor who specializes in a subject such as computer books and is therefore familiar with the markets for books on the subject.

Stress those groups of people who buy books. For instance, your book may be of interest to minorities, the elderly, or the handicapped, but stressing these groups won't help sell your proposal because publishers do not perceive them as important book buyers.

Women buy most books, so a book that caters to them has a head start.

If it's not clear to you what kinds of consumers buy the kind of book you are writing, ask your bookseller or librarian.

Specialty Stores

Next, list specialty stores such as gourmet shops, music, sporting goods, hardware, or stationery stores that sell similar books. Check with stores to see if they can sell your book. If they can, ask them how many such stores there are in the country or how you can find that number, and how they buy their books. You will find relatively few books in specialty stores, but if your book has that potential, passing this information along will impress an editor with your thoroughness.

Course Adoptions

If your book will have adoption potential in schools or other institutions, identify the courses and academic levels for which it will be suitable. Naming professors at different schools who are eager to adopt your book will go over well.

Special Sales

Finally, cover special sales markets for your book. These are bulk sales to corporations or institutions which might buy large quantities of your book for internal use or to sell at a reduced price or to use as a promotional giveaway.

A savings and loan in our neighborhood once gave away a series of Bantam's ethnic cookbooks over a period of time to encourage prospective savers to start accounts. A corporation might buy copies of a book on business writing for its employees.

This kind of sale is more likely with a paperback than a hard cover, and more likely with a mass-market book than a more expensive trade paperback. Noting what kinds of companies use books and discussing this possibility with friends who know marketing will help you decide if your book can generate special sales. Only a small percentage of books are used this way, so don't spend much time investigating it unless you can deliver a sale yourself. Major publishers have sales departments for exploring special sales.

10. Subsidiary Rights

Your publisher will retain the right to sell your book to book clubs, so suggest which clubs might be interested in it. *Literary Market Place*, which is in your library, includes a list of clubs.

Briefly speculate on other subsidiary rights sales the project may generate: film, foreign, first serial, merchandising (items such as T-shirts), software, audio and videocassettes, and other ways to exploit the commercial potential of your book in other than book form. If you have an agent or plan to use the proposal to find one, the agent may want to keep these rights for you, but mentioning them will add to the editor's sense of excitement about the project's potential.

This is what John Markoff and Lenny Siegel wrote about foreign sales of their book: "The international market for *Where the Chips May Fall* is potentially significant. There is widespread interest in silicon technology and its social impact in major industrial countries like England, France, Germany, and Japan."

The proposal for *Home Before Morning: The Story of a Nurse in Vietnam* noted that "the authors' agents have received offers from producers interested in making a film of Lynda's life."

Merchandising rights usually come into play with certain kinds of books, such as humor books, with an important graphic element that lends itself to translation into other forms and media. Usually only bestsellers have created the recognition needed for merchandising sales. Kliban's cats and Jim Davis's Garfield, for instance, found their way onto cups, towels, and other products.

Reading Paul Nathan's column, "Rights and Permissions," in *Publishers Weekly* will keep you abreast of what kinds of rights are being sold, by whom, and for how much. Also keep your eye out for products derived from books and get into the habit of thinking creatively about how to resell your book in forms other than between covers.

11. Spin-offs

Neither editors nor agents want literary one-night stands. They would much rather discover a writer than a book. Writers who can be counted on to turn out a book or more a year can become valuable properties.

If you can develop the book into a series of similar books on the same subject or with the same structure, begin this section with the statement: "If (title) is successful, the author will write a series of books on x covering A, B, and C."

Will your book lend itself to sequels or spin-offs?

If you're going to write a book for adults, is a children's or young-adult version possible?

If you're planning a book that can be adopted for a college course, can you write other versions that can be used in elementary, high school, graduate school, or the growing field of continuing education?

If you're writing a book for men, are variations for women and children possible?

If it's an introductory book, should there be an intermediate or advanced version?

If your book is directed to corporate types, would it also be useful to entrepreneurs and nonprofit groups?

In short, how many ways can your idea be recycled in book form? Mention them even if you don't want to write them. They will help prove the book's commercial potential.

If you plan to pursue the possibility of a radio or television show or a daily or weekly newspaper or magazine column based on the book, and have the background or credits to make such a possibility likely, say so.

Radio and television spin-offs of books are unusual, but books often lend themselves to other books on the same subject or with the same structure. Jay Levinson's *Earning Money Without a Job* included a series of ideas for working for oneself. This led to Jay's book *555 Ways to Earn Extra Money*, which in turn led to a syndicated column called "Earning Extra Money."

12. Promotion

When you get to this point in the Overview, explain how you think the publisher can promote the book and how you will help. Your ideas should be creative and effective, but not costly. As long as you don't give the impression of being on an ego trip, editors will welcome your eagerness to promote your book.

If, for instance, your book will lend itself to print and broadcast publicity, mention it. If you can travel to other cities as a lecturer, for example—in other words, send yourself on a publicity tour—list the cities you will go to. Unless yours will be a major book, assume your publisher will not send you on tour. But if they know you will be traveling to different cities, their publicity department ought to be willing to approach local media about interviews.

Describe classes you teach or personal appearances at which you can sell the book. If you can sell 500 or more copies a year, state the number.

List well-known writers, experts, or celebrities you will contact for quotes for the cover of the book.

HOT TIP *The moment you decide to write your book, start a promotion file. As ideas pop into your head, jot them down and file them. Developed into an imaginative plan for promoting your book, these ideas will help sell your proposal.*

---

13. Competitive Books

Once you've told editors everything you think they should know about your book, it's time to make use of the data you gathered when you researched competitive books and assuage their fear about the competition. You will accelerate the decision-making process if you do their market research for them by reviewing competitive books.

List them in order of importance, supplying the full title, author, publisher, year of publication, number of pages, and price. This information should not read like the card file at the library: Put authors' first names first, omitting publishers' locations and the word *Inc*.

Then in two phrases or sentences, indicate first what each book includes, then its shortcomings. At the end of this list, include a statement summarizing the differences between your book and its predecessors, making it clear why yours will be "the" book on the subject.

Be factual and don't sound self-serving when noting the deficiencies of competitive books or the virtues of yours. Assume the editor either has seen or knows about them. Will your book be more thorough, timely, beautiful, comprehensive, or up-to-date than its predecessors? If you think your book will be better written, your proposal must prove it.

Pamphlets, scholarly books from academic presses, and professional books from specialized publishers, such as those for doctors, lawyers, and real estate salespeople, don't count as competition because of their limited bookstore distribution, so don't include them. Don't include out-of-print or religious titles that won't appeal to the general public. Editors are concerned about bookseller and buyer resistance to your book caused by similar books that have national distribution to bookstores. These books may turn up on bookstore shelves next to yours or may even have satisfied readers' curiosity about the subject.

At the same time, as mentioned earlier, the success of books on the same subject that won't compete with yours will convince an editor of the market for books on the subject. If the books aren't well known, indicate what they contain. If you are preparing your proposal for a specific publisher, be sure to mention their complementary books. This list doesn't have to be exhaustive, just convincing. Close with a statement on how the existence of these books proves the salability of yours.

HOT TIP *You have only one chance to lose your credibility as a writer and an authority. One egregious error, in style or content, and everything you write will be suspect. Make your facts and your prose unassailable. Aristotle taught that every line in a play should develop the atmosphere, the characters, or the plot, and, if possible, all three. Every word is either helping or hurting your chances of selling your proposal. You must become sensitive to the use of every word, and if anything isn't pulling its weight, drop it. Don't weaken your proposal or waste an editor's time. Like the final manuscript, your proposal should not contain an extra word, person, action, fact, or idea.*

Once you have completed the 13 steps of the Overview and proved you have a salable idea, it's time to prove that you have made a realistic assessment of the resources you need to complete the project, including the most important resource of all: you.

Resources Needed to Complete the Book

On a separate page entitled "Resources Needed to Complete the Book," describe the out-of-pocket expenses, starting with the largest, that will affect the size of the advance that you need to finish the book.

Your largest expense may be travel. If you write that you need a certain sum for a trip, a publisher may offer that sum. If you just mention the trip, you may get a larger offer. Be specific about where you're going and how long you'll be there. For example: "Researching the book will require a two-week trip to New York." If why you're going isn't obvious, explain it.

Include round but specific figures for artwork, photography, an introduction, accessing data bases, and permissions to use quotes or illustrations. Give the total for each kind of expense, not an item-by-item breakdown, for instance: "The book's photography budget will be $500."

Don't mention small items like the cost of office supplies, but if an expense like long-distance phone calls or a combination of expenses will run $500 or more, include the cost.

If you are not planning to type the book yourself, include the cost for having the manuscript typed.

If there are more than three sums involved, they will be easier to read if, after describing them, you list them in column form with the type of expense on the left, the costs on the right, and a total at the bottom of the list. For example: Completion of the book will require a permissions budget of $1,000, 15 photographs costing $650, long-distance calls totaling $500, and a typist for $750:

Permissions	$1,000
Photographs	650
Telephone calls	500
Typing	750
TOTAL:	$2,900

If your expenses are self-explanatory, as in the sample proposal, you can write the resource page in the form of a list.

Usually it is the author's responsibility to pay for expenses involved in researching and writing a book, including the permissions costs, and the publisher's job to take it from there. Publishers may, however, provide a separate advance for large expenses, and, if they want a book badly enough, they will pay for part or all of the expenses. Failing that, they may provide a separate advance for expenses.

Permissions

Permissions grant you the right to excerpt copyrighted material—a passage, a page, a chapter, or a short story—in your book. Quotes of fewer than 250 words from a book are usually considered "fair use," that is, they may be used without permission of the copyright holder. To avoid problems, obtain written permission for all quotes.

To establish the cost of permissions to use quotes and illustrations from books, look up the publishers in *Literary Market Place*, and contact the rights and permissions person. For permissions on material not in books, contact the copyright holder. If someone is reluctant to quote a figure unless you know who the publisher will be, and the format, price, and first printing of the book, try to get a price range for your estimate.

Ask for the price for the United States and Canada. This is the basic grant of rights your publisher will expect to buy. In general, the cost for world English-language rights which will be needed for an English edition will be one-third of the cost of American and Canadian rights. Depending on who retains foreign rights, you or your publisher can arrange for permissions for an English edition and translations when it becomes necessary.

If you're doing an anthology, or obtaining the right to use copyrighted material is essential to writing the book, or you expect the cost of permissions to run more than $1,000, find out as much as you can about permissions for your proposal. Make sure if you can that the copyright holder will let you use the material, and that even if you can't determine it precisely, the cost won't be prohibitive. Learning everything you can now may prevent you from proposing quotes or illustrations you can't get or can't afford.

If you're just using a few quotes which you can omit or find substitutes for, then just mention that completing the book will require permissions costs for x quotes or illustrations.

Permissions costs may be a bargaining chip in negotiating your contract. Since your publisher may be willing to pay for part or all of the permissions, or give you a separate advance for them, or even handle the paperwork on them, it is to your advantage to provide at least a ballpark figure for the cost.

Wrapping a Package

If you're proposing an illustrated book and you want to package it, that is, provide either a copy-edited manuscript ready to be typeset, or a camera-ready mechanical, or bound books, include the costs involved and your experience as a packager along with the publishing experience of your colleagues. Unless you're only willing to sell the project if you can package it, suggest this as an option, since the publisher may prefer to take care of the editing, design, and production. Suggest this only if you have had packaging experience.

HOT TIP *Unless your book will be very complicated to do or is large in scope, it's not necessary to explain how you will research it. The proposal should prove that you know what you're doing. If an agent or editor is working with another writer on a similar project, valuable information may wind up in a competitor's hands. If editors have questions about your research techniques, they'll ask.*

Two exceptions: If your book requires access to celebrities or VIPs, show that you have it. If you're planning a biography, indicate your access to the person. If the subject is dead, note whether the bio will be authorized and whether the estate is giving you access to the person's papers.

Dollars and Sense

Although it will not be part of your proposal, draw up a complete budget of your personal and writing expenses. Keep in mind that publishers regard an advance as a sum of money enabling a writer to meet expenses involved in writing a book. How you pay the rent is your problem. Naturally you want enough money so you can devote all of your time to completing your book, and editors know that the smaller the advance, the more time it may take for you to turn in the manuscript.

HOT TIP *If your advance won't cover your expenses, try to get writing assignments that will take you where you need to go so that between selling assigned articles or articles based on the book, you may be able to make up the difference.*

Timing Yourself

The time it takes you to research and write the proposal, particularly the sample chapters, will give you a reasonably reliable basis on which to judge how long it will take you to write the rest of the book.

Also try this: Once you have finished your proposal, go through your outline chapter by chapter, and using the time you spent on the sample chapters as a criterion, guess how long it will take you to do each chapter, then tote up the results.

Publishers want to start recouping their investments as soon as possible. They also want their books well written. Don't commit yourself to writing 50,000 words in two months or an editor will not believe you're going to do a professional job.

The time you allot should make sense in relation to your ability, the time it takes to write the sample chapters, and the book's subject and length. After you decide how long the book will take, give yourself a month or two as a cushion to allow for unexpected problems which force you to veer off course. Six months, nine months, and a year are common deadlines. Yours should be what you feel will enable you to produce your best work.

Ideally, publishers would like to publish a book and have it sell forever without having to change it. And they are reluctant to do books that have to be updated every year, unless, like almanacs, consumer guides, or books on taxes, a large readership is waiting for them.

If your book holds the promise of continuing sales but will require updating, indicate how often you will do it, and don't include anything in the book that will become outdated before the revision. The fewer the revisions, the easier it will be on the publisher and on you.

If the information on resources only runs a paragraph, add it to the end of the Overview. The last sentence about resources is this: "The manuscript will be finished x months after the receipt of the advance." If time is the only resource you need, then this is the only sentence you will need about resources.

If you already have a partial or complete manuscript, the last sentence on resources should read: "X chapters of the book are finished in draft form and the rest of the book will be completed x months after receipt of the advance" or "The manuscript is complete in draft form."

If you are proposing a series, add when, and if it's not clear, in what order you will deliver the rest of the manuscripts.

Chin Up

If it sounds as if you have to know everything about your book before you have fully researched it, relax. What you have to do is convince editors that you know your subject, that you're giving them an opportunity to latch on to a winner, and that you can write it.

Editors understand that you are presenting the book only on the basis of what you know now. Once the project is sold, you and the editor will have an identical interest in producing the best possible book, and you will be free to improve on what you propose in any way that you and the editor agree will help the book. But a well-thought-out proposal may save you grief later by ensuring that you are writing the same book the editor is buying.

You don't have to be an expert on the subject when you begin researching it. Starting a proposal with just an open mind and a passionate, insatiable curiosity is better than setting out with misconceptions or prejudices. Another joy of the writing life is the opportunity to learn new things that enable you to grow both as a person and as a professional.

After you've finished the proposal, you will probably know more about the subject than an agent or editor. Your research will elevate you toward the status of an expert. The bio that follows should prove that you're a pro.

About the Author

What qualifies you to write this book? Answer this question on the last page of the Introduction, "About the Author," by describing in descending order of relevance and importance everything about you that will prove you can write and promote the book.

Avoid the extremes of false humility or hype, and keeping in mind that most of us have led one-page lives, include every facet of your personal and professional experience that adds luster to you as a person and a writer: published work, jobs, years of research, education, awards, travel, special skills. If your qualifications are unique and you didn't mention them in your Overview, now's the time.

If you have had a book published, give the title, publisher, and year. Indicate book and subsidiary rights sales if they are substantial. Unless you've received raves in major periodicals, editors won't take the time to read complete reviews. Extract favorable quotes. If the editor is not likely to be familiar with the source of the quote, describe the periodical and include the circulation if it's impressive.

If your book was blessed with a half page or more of quotes, put them in descending order of importance on a separate page with the heading: "From the Reviews of (title)." If your book did receive outstanding reviews in important magazines or newspapers, underline the good parts and enclose the review after the proposal.

Name the periodicals in which your work has appeared; the number of years you've been writing or researching the subject; the number of articles you've had published and the range of subjects you've written about if you think these figures will impress an editor. If you've written articles about the subject of the book, specify when and for whom.

HOT TIP *If you are a writer, don't use a résumé. Résumés contain information editors don't need and they're too formal. You may be applying for work, but you're not applying for a job. Make your bio a clear, concise, simple, no-nonsense description of your life and work.*

If you are a professor or an artist out to impress an editor with your credentials and not your writing, a résumé format will do. Again, list your achievements in descending order of relevance and importance and only include what an editor needs to know.

Write your bio in the third person as if you were writing a news release about yourself. Editors will appreciate your modesty and it will read better than a page full of I's.

However, the energy and commitment needed for a book are so great that your desire to write it must be strong enough to weather whatever vicissitudes fate has in store for you. So if you wish, at the end of your bio, take the opportunity to convey your passion for the project. If you do, write your bio in the first person but remember that unless you are writing your book in the first person, this will be the only place in the proposal where you should use the word *I*.

Indicate the exposure you've had in the media, especially in connection with the subject of the book. Including an article about yourself with the significant points underlined, particularly if it's also about the subject of the book, will prove the acceptance of you and your idea in the media. A story with a photo is a plus. If you want to use more than one article, place the articles at the end of the proposal or in the second pocket of the folder recommended in the section on how to submit your proposal.

Whether or not you've had experience doing interviews, mention your willingness to do publicity.

Point out your background as a speaker or teacher, or experience with promotion that will help you help the publisher push your opus.

Describe connections you have in business, government, the media, or your profession who can be counted on to promote the book.

Discuss other books you plan to write. As I've noted, agents and publishers are anxious to discover authors who can be counted on to turn out a book or more a year. Limit your description to one line of copy for no more than three books. You might even wind up selling a book you're thinking of writing instead of the one you propose.

If you've joined the computer revolution, mention the model, word-processing program, and disks you use.

If you have a family, mention it, along with where you live.

Letting your personality come through in your bio without being intrusive is fine, especially if it will help sell the proposal or promote the book. However, cute is out, as are humor (unless you're writing a humor book), far-out approaches to telling your life story, and sympathy for the devil, uhh, editor, as in "I know that many books pass your desk, but. . . ." (See what I mean about being cute?)

Here is Michelle Saadi's biography:

Michelle Saadi spent three years as a personal injury claims adjuster with one of the country's largest auto insurance companies. She investigated and settled nearly 500 accidents, handling everything from minor whiplashes to disabling nerve injuries, learning every tactic used to cheat accident victims. After leaving the company, she decided to use her experience to write *Claiming Your Share*.

Although this will be Saadi's first book, she has done technical writing and editing for several engineering firms. In addition, she has written articles on animal welfare and has debated the issue. Saadi is at ease in dealing with the media and speaking out on controversial issues. She believes that radio and television interviews will be helpful in publicizing *Claiming Your Share* and she feels that she will be an asset in promoting the book.

Saadi was born and raised in Los Angeles, graduating from UCLA with a B.A. in psychology. She lives in San Jose.

Elizabeth Pomada's bio is an example of a passionate first-person bio:

The author Anna Chapin once wrote: "Many a place gets into your mind and creates nostalgia when you are far from it. But Greenwich Village gets into your heart, and you will never be quite able to lose the magic of it all the days of your life."

I headed for Greenwich Village upon graduation from Cornell University. I lived at 24 West 12th Street, a gracious brownstone mansion known as Rosemary House, following the footsteps of an aunt who did the same thing when she graduated from Cornell in 1936. The house, a National Historic Landmark, was built in 1851 for Civil War hero General Winfield Scott.

Although I worked uptown, I went to the New School for Social Research up the block in the evening, and the Fifth Avenue Cinema around the corner. Many a paycheck went right to Dauber & Pine, the musty ark of a bookstore on Fifth Avenue between 12th and 13th Streets, and many a weekend afternoon was spent sitting in Washington Square or wandering the wonderful back streets.

I am the author of dozens of articles on art, travel, and books which have appeared in shelter and national and local consumer magazines. My first book, *California Publicity Outlets*, for which I made 2,500 phone calls to list the personnel of California's 1,700 newspapers, magazines, radio and television stations, was published by Unicorn Systems Company in 1972. It's still distributed as *Metro California Media* by New York Publicity Outlets.

Places to Go with Children in Northern California was published by Chronicle Books in 1973; a newly designed, completely revised edition was published in May 1980. I ghosted Dinesh Bahadur's *Come Fight a Kite*, published by Harvey House in 1978, and was co-author of Dutton's *Painted Ladies: San Francisco's Resplendent Victorians*, which now has 60,000 copies in print.

I live in San Francisco—after working in publishing at Holt, Rinehart & Winston, David McKay, and Dial—and am a partner in Michael Larsen/Elizabeth Pomada Literary Agents.

Writing *America's Left Bank* will bring me full circle, giving form to the Greenwich Village magic that's always been in my heart.

If, judging from the author interviews you see, you think that your looks will be an asset in promoting the book, affix an 8" x 10" black-and-white photo of yourself on the page after your bio. A high-quality photocopy will be acceptable if you're submitting more than one copy of the proposal.

If you are sharing authorship with a writer, photographer, or illustrator, each of you should have a separate page for your bios.

If you are submitting a complete manuscript or a self-published book, you don't have to prepare anything described beyond this point, but you should include an Overview, information on future expenses such as artwork and permissions, and a bio.

It may take you a lot of time and effort to get to this point in your proposal, yet the three parts of your Overview may add up to only five pages. The next challenge is to prove that, like a farmer who's picked a basket of cotton, you can use the raw data you've gathered to spin out a bookful of information that's worth putting between covers. On to the outline!

CHAPTER THREE

The Chapter-by-Chapter Outline

The proposal's next challenge is to prove that there's a book's worth of information in the idea and that you have created the structure which best suits the subject. A chapter-by-chapter outline, sometimes called an annotated table of contents, enables the editor and you to envision the finished manuscript.

What? No Outline?

Certain kinds of books such as cartoon books or picture books may not lend themselves to being outlined. But editors are more sanguine about a project if it has a unifying theme and structure.

When I wrote the proposal for *Painted Ladies*, instead of just proposing a book of photographs of houses, I gave the book a structure by dividing it into four sections covering different parts of the city. Later, as we were doing the book, we added another kind of form to the book by arranging the photographs in the order of an architectural tour.

Someday somebody is going to do a coffee-table book called *The Art of Reading*. This could be no more than the most beautiful paintings in history of people reading books. But if the pictures were arranged in chronological order, and the text not only described the art but speculated about the people who were reading, what they were reading, and what the world of books and publishing was like at the time, the book would become a cultural history.

Again, the point is, if possible, to impose some kind of form on your idea. Reading the outline instructions may stimulate some ideas.

Two Simplified Outlines

1. If your book will consist of a series of chapters, each with the same structure and presenting the same kind of information, you don't have to prepare the in-depth outline called for below. Just list the chapters and

then list what each will contain. This simplified outline would follow the fourth item in the Overview on the length of the book.

For example, if you were going to write a buyers' guide to classic cars or a guidebook to Europe's ten greatest cities, you would list in order the cars or cities the book will cover, then also in order list the aspects of the cars or cities the book will cover.

2. If you are planning a compilation of information such as an almanac, a dictionary, or an encyclopedia, just list in order the topics the book will include after your Overview. For Dianna Crowe's dictionary for investors, *How to Talk Money*, and for Arthur Naiman's *Every Goy's Guide to Common Jewish Expressions*, the authors provided an alphabetical list of entries.

Hide and Go Seek

Michelangelo believed that his statues were waiting for him inside the blocks of marble he assaulted with hammer and chisel. Imagine that you are a sculptor and that the first conception of your idea is an enormous block of marble. Inside it is a magnificent edifice, a majestic cathedral, the perfect embodiment of your idea. Your job is to use your vision, skills, and tools to construct a sturdy foundation and chip away the superfluous until only a beautiful, flawless structure in which form and function are inseparable remains.

The outline is not a showcase for you to dazzle editors with your style, but rather to show how well you can research, organize, and outline the book in about a dozen pages or less. Though the outline needn't be a stylistic triumph, it should read well. Providing a sound structure for the individual chapters and for the book as a whole demonstrates a firm grasp of the subject and how best to translate it into book form.

A skimpy outline will have editors asking themselves: "Sure it's a great idea, but how do I know it's a book and not just an article?" A thin outline also invites problems from the unexpected. By not thoroughly investigating what's involved in writing the book, you are more likely to encounter more books to read, places to go, people to interview, illustrations or quotes to obtain than you had reckoned on.

You must do enough research to write a solid outline. The more complete your outline is, the less likely you are to be unpleasantly surprised by what you discover as you research the book.

Opening Lines

The first page of the outline should start with the heading "The Chapter-by-Chapter Outline," and underneath it should be a double-spaced list of the chapter titles and the pages on which each chapter outline begins.

Give each chapter a title as provocative or as clear as the book's title. If you wish, give chapters catchy or intriguing titles, but then use subtitles to tell readers what the chapter is about. In addition to giving an editor a feeling for the flow and structure of the book, the list of chapter titles, like the menu at the Four Seasons, should whet the editor's appetite for what follows.

An alternative to subtitles is to begin the outline with a one-sentence overview of the chapter. Here are three ways to start this sentence:

```
This chapter...

The goal (aim, purpose, object) of this chapter is to...

This chapter is divided into (consists of) x parts which...
```

The last alternative has the added virtue of telling the editor about the structure of the chapter.

Here are the first sentences of the outlines for two chapters in Michael Lillyquist's *Sunlight & Health: The Positive and Negative Effects of the Sun on You*, which suggest other ways of starting a chapter outline:

The second chapter serves as an introduction to current knowledge about the nature of sunlight and its effects on us.
The final chapter addresses the advances civilization has made with the advent of artificial lighting as well as the problems encountered.

Outlining a chapter with a series of one-line topics set off with letters or numbers looks academic and doesn't reveal enough about the chapter. So *starting each chapter outline on a new page*, describe concisely the contents of the chapter: the instructions in a how-to book, the characters and events in a history or biography, the development of a book's thesis.

A page of prose for every chapter will make a solid, impressive out line, but a chapter outline may run from one paragraph to two pages or more, depending on the kind of book you're writing, how much informa tion you have, and how long the chapter will be. For most books, howev er, a page or less of outline for each chapter is enough. Write the outline your book calls for. If your book requires chapter outlines of a half a page or less, type the outlines one after the other instead of putting each chap ter on a separate page.

Outline every chapter, including those you submit as sample chapters, so an editor can see how the chapters flow into one another, how the book as a whole will hang together, and how a page of outline relates to a completed chapter.

If you want the book to start with an introduction about whatever you want readers to know before launching into the text, outline it just as you would a separate chapter. Since the introduction may be shorter than a chapter, the outline for it may also be shorter. In their haste to dive into the book, readers may skip the introduction, so write about the book, not the subject. If the subject requires an introduction, make it the first or second chapter.

If you plan to divide the book into several parts, each with three or four chapters, give these parts titles, and if it will help readers, do a short introduction to each part. Outline in a paragraph what the introduction to each part will contain.

HOT TIP   *The Golden Rule of writing an outline: Write about the chapter, not about the subject.*

Getting Started

The beginning of a chapter outline should look like this:

```
Part X  (on the first page of each part)

Chapter X

Title of the Chapter                    x pages, x photos
```

Writing the sample chapters will give you a working sense of the relationship between outline and manuscript. As you write the sample chapters, develop a sense of how a page of outline corresponds to the finished chapter.

After you have written the sample chapters and completed your outlines, go through the outlines paragraph by paragraph, and based on your experience of how the outlines evolved into sample chapters, estimate how many pages of manuscript each paragraph of the outlines will become. It will usually be clear whether a paragraph in the outline will turn into three, five, seven, ten, or more pages. You'll get the knack of it as you do it.

The length of a chapter may range from 15 to 35 manuscript pages. Fewer than 15 pages will seem slight, and once a chapter starts running longer than 35 pages, consider dividing it into two chapters.

Twenty to 25 pages is a reasonable chapter length for most nonfiction, but the length will vary depending on the subject of the chapter and the nature of the book. Yet even if a chapter is only 15 pages, it is usually possible to supply an editor with one page of information about it.

When you add up the number of illustrations and pages in the chapters and combine them with the page count of the back matter, you will obtain the figures you need for the book hook in the Overview.

However difficult this may seem, keep in mind that besides impressing the publisher, you're doing yourself a favor. The outline is a writing tool as well as a selling tool. You will definitely feel more confident once you've finished a couple of chapters and are armed with a clear vision of the rest of the book.

When you mention a person, place, event, fact, or instruction you plan to illustrate, add the word *photo, graph, map, drawing,* or *chart* after it in parentheses. An alternative is to skip a line after the end of the outline, type the word *Illustrations,* then list them in paragraph form in the order they will appear.

Again, editors know you are guessing, and you'll be free to make changes in what you propose. But editors react favorably to proposals that present a firm, specific approach to every aspect of the book.

Another opportunity to be specific occurs whenever a chapter will cover a number of related events, ideas, facts, or techniques. Instead of using the word *several,* say, for example, *four techniques.* If you have space on the page, list them. If parts of a list consist of five or more words, they will be easier to read and remember if you type each part of the list on a separate, indented, double-spaced line.

Identify sources of quotes. If the book, person, or periodical is not well known, include additional information such as a date, place, or circumstance, to place the quote in a meaningful context. For the same reason, if you mention a person or incident, include enough information so an editor understands what you're writing about and why.

Avoid raising unanswered questions. Asking questions editors can't answer doesn't help your cause, so avoid questions altogether in the Overview and outline. The purpose of the proposal is not to ask questions, but to *answer* every question an editor may have about you and your book. The only part of the proposal in which questions make sense is the sample material, in which you're free to address the reader.

Making Outlines Read Like Outlines

If you simply summarize your chapters, the outline will read like an article, and you will run a serious risk that editors will reject your proposal, thinking that the idea doesn't have enough substance for a book.

Here are two suggestions for making your chapter outlines read like outlines instead of summaries:

1. Give each chapter a structure.

You will find one of these three approaches effective:

• Divide a chapter into parts that become the organization of the chapter and can also be mentioned in the title of the chapter. For example: "Four Reasons Why You Should Quit Smoking."

The title of Chapter 8 in Michelle Saadi's book is:

"Claiming Your Share: Eight Steps to a Successful Settlement."

• A second technique is to structure each chapter with a beginning, middle, and end. Indicate this structure by introducing each part of the chapter. Following are alternative openings for the successive parts of a chapter:

```
First, the chapter...

The first (opening) part (section, segment) of the chapter...

The chapter begins (starts, opens with)...

...starts (begins, opens) the chapter.

In the opening part (section, segment) of the chapter...

Next (at this point) in the chapter is (comes)...

The next (following, middle) part (segment, section) of the chapter...

In the following (next, middle) section (part, segment) of the chapter...

...follows (comes next).

The chapter's next (middle) section (segment)...

Finally, the chapter...

The last (final, closing, concluding) part of the chapter...

The rest of the chapter...

The chapter ends (concludes, closes) with...

...ends (concludes, completes) the chapter.

In the last (final, closing, concluding) part of the chapter...

The chapter's conclusion...
```

This is the outline for Chapter 2 of *Claiming Your Share:*

Chapter 2

First Contacts:

How to Steal a Claim on the First Visit   25 pages

This chapter analyzes the techniques adjusters use to manipulate accident victims into early settlements of their claims. It is divided into three sections.

The first part describes the cultivated image of adjusters and their tactic of making unannounced visits to a claimant's home. This introduces the concept of jury appeal and its devastating impact on handicapped, minority, and unattractive claimants.

Case histories document the pressure adjusters use to force poor and uneducated claimants into quick, cheap settlements. An explanation of whiplash injuries expands this discussion and illustrates the methods used to manipulate victims into settling before they realize they are seriously hurt. This section ends with an examination of settlements made by telephone and releases that are tape-recorded instead of being signed.

The next segment presents recommendations for claimants to help them counter these tactics. These include seeing a doctor immediately, refraining from strenuous physical activity, and documenting the emergency nature of any physical labor.

The second part of the chapter continues with advice on how and where to see an adjuster, with emphasis on minorities and the handicapped. An anecdote that illustrates actions that indigent victims can take to protect themselves ends this section.

The final part of the chapter discusses the justifications and methods for reopening claims settled too soon or for too little money. It includes information to gather before seeing a lawyer, a look at

```
which claims are easiest to reopen, and case histories with special

instructions for minorities.  The chapter closes with a strong warning

about the dangers of first-call settlements.
```

• The third way to arrive at a chapter structure is to try to conceptualize the information in the book and in each chapter in the form of an image or symbol which will both clarify the gist of the chapter in a unifying, memorable way and provide the structure for the chapter.

Is it possible to visualize the material in your book or a chapter of it as a shape like a circle, or a pie, the slices of which constitute the substance of the chapter? Could the information be compared to a plant (remember *Roots?*), an activity, a machine, a person, a place, a period or event in history? Like an evocative title for a book, the right image can convey the tone and structure of a chapter.

For example, my book about literary agents has separate chapters about a terrible day and a terrific day in the life of an agent. Starting in the morning, I made up a composite of the horrible and wonderful things that have befallen our agency over the years.

The search for the proper structure for your chapters and your book is another example of how reading comparable books may get your creative juices flowing.

2. Use "outline" verbs that tell what the chapter does.

For instance, instead of writing a description of the Left Bank in Paris, write: "The next part of the chapter portrays the Left Bank in Paris. . . ."

To give you a better feeling for outline verbs, here is an alphabetical potpourri of them culled from *Roget's II: The New Thesaurus* (Houghton Mifflin), a handy resource to check if you find yourself stuck for the right word. You don't have to read the list now, but it will be helpful as you prepare your outline.

address	argue	build (on, up)
advance	assert	center (on, around)
advise	assess	challenge
advocate	attack	clarify
affirm	balance	complete
agree	blast	confirm
analyze	blend	confront
appraise	broaden	continue

convince
debunk
defend
define
deliver
demonstrate
deplore
describe
detail
develop
discuss
dispel
dissect
distill
document
dramatize
elaborate
emphasize
enable
encourage
establish
evaluate
examine
expand
explain
explore
expose
express
focus on
follow
forge
form
give (voice to)
go (into, on, over, through)
hammer
harmonize
help
identify
illuminate

illustrate
include
incorporate
integrate
introduce
investigate
join
judge
justify
lay out
lead to
link
list
lock horns
look
maintain
mark
marshal
mention
move on to
name
narrow
note
offer
outline
paint
pepper
persuade
pinpoint
place (in perspective)
point out
portray
prescribe
present
proceed (with, by)
prod
prompt
propose
prove
provide

puncture
put (an end to, before, in perspective, into context)
question
raise
recommend
recount
refute
reject
relate
remind
reply
report
resolve
respond
reveal
review
say
scrutinize
set (forth, up)
shake up
share
shift
show
sort out
specify
speculate
stimulate
strive
suggest
summarize
supply
support
surprise
tackle
take (advantage of, a look at, issue with, on, place, up)
talk

tease	unify	venture
teem	unmask	vindicate
tell	unravel	voice
thrill	unveil	warn
tie (together, up)	uphold	wax
uncover	urge	weed out
undertake	use	widen
unearth	(give) vent (to)	work out

To expand the list, try adding the prefixes dis-, re-, or un-; see if the opposite of a verb fits, or if you can use it as a noun.

HOT TIP *Write about the book in the future tense, and write the outline in the present tense. The outline will contain many verbs; it will read better without all those "wills."*

If you employ the same verbs too often, the outline reads like a formula. Avoid using the same verb twice in the same chapter or more than four times in the outline. If you use a verb more than once, vary its form. You can use many of the verbs above in three ways: "the middle section of the chapter reveals," "begins by revealing," or "begins with the revelation that . . . ." Vary verbs as much as accuracy allows.

You can use verbs that involve readers or characters:

```
The chapter opens by encouraging (warning) readers to...

The following section takes (leads) the reader to...

In the last part of the chapter, the reader learns (discovers, finds

out, meets, sees)...
```

If you're writing about people, you are free to use verbs that describe their actions. In a biography, however, avoid a string of sentences beginning with *he* or *she*.

Avoid the passive voice:

Wrong:
The issue of drunk drivers is examined.
Right:
Next, the chapter examines the issue of drunk drivers.

If you have trouble preparing the outline, first list the bare bones of the chapter and the topics it covers, fleshing them out later with connective tissue.

The Question of Time

Maintain continuity within and between chapters so there is a natural, graceful progression of ideas, incidents, and information. If the story unfolds over time, include enough dates so an editor can keep track of time.

If you are writing about a person, historical period, issue, system, or endeavor, the subject will have a past. Put its past into context by providing a historical perspective. By the end of the outline, an editor should have a clear sense of continuity in the subject's past, present, and future.

This doesn't mean that you have to start at the beginning. Consider following the epic tradition of starting *in medias res*, in the middle of things, with a powerhouse first chapter which hooks the reader with as much intensity as you can muster. Then you can backtrack to place the story in perspective.

Besides placing your subject in the context of time, also establish its geographical context, its relevance, if any, to what is happening in the field elsewhere in America and the world. This will be an expansion of the perspective you gave the editor in the subject hook in your Overview.

The outline should be so teeming with facts and ideas that editors will easily be able to visualize the proposal expanded into a full-length manuscript and be delighted at the prospect.

Two Right Hooks

Always look for the hook. Start each chapter with the right hook—a quote, event, anecdote, statistic, idea, surprise, or joke—to grab the reader's interest. Try to end chapters with a hook or climax to induce readers to turn the page to the next chapter. If you don't include the hook itself in the outline, describe it.

If you can, begin or end a chapter with something compelling that is also new. In fact, as you outline the book, if you are presenting a new idea for the first time and if it's not clear, mention it. The new elements in your book help justify its existence.

If you come across an informative or entertaining quote or anecdote that captures the essence of the chapter, put it, along with the source, at the beginning of the outline, setting it off from the text by indenting it. You can also use a short passage of dialogue from a biography or a book about history. But don't use something in the outline if it will appear in a sample chapter.

Here is how Joanne Wilkens started the outline for the third chapter of her 62-page proposal for *Women: The New Entrepreneurs:*

> Enough! I'm tired of waiting. If they won't make me a president, I'll make myself a president.
> —Jayne Townsend, Jayne Townsend and Associates, Ltd., a management consulting firm

> The company I worked for was doing poorly. I watched the boss lose money and knew I could do it better.
> —Carol Hayes, age 43, landscape architect

This chapter will be the first in the literature to examine why women decide to go into business for themselves.

Joanne began a chapter called "No Money, No Credit, No Business" with a quote that is also an anecdote:

> My business was self-supporting when I started so I didn't need any loan. After three or four years, I wanted a $5,000 line of credit so I took my tax returns to the bank. You could see that I was making more money every year, but the loan officer treated me very shabbily. I never felt like such a nothing. . . .
> —Marion Lee, age 52, owner, import-export firm

In his 71-page proposal for *The Insider's Guide to Health Foods,* David Armstrong begins a chapter titled "For Appearance's Sake Only: 'Natural, Organic' Cosmetics" like this: "The 17 listed ingredients in Clairol's Herbal Essence shampoos include synthetic preservatives, artificial colors, emulsifiers, a detergent, and unspecified herbs identified only as 'fragrance.' Yet the product is marketed as 'natural.' "

Heads Up

As this book illustrates, separating sections of text with subheads breaks up an endless procession of paragraphs. Subheads will also make your outline easier to read, and if they're clever, they will engage the editor's interest in what follows. Since subheads will be part of the manuscript, they can address the reader.

To provide unity and continuity in the outline, begin and end chapters with introductory and concluding remarks, and end the book with a closing statement summing up the book.

This is the outline for a chapter from Elizabeth Pomada's *America's Left Bank:*

Bohemia in All its Glory 1900-1916   38 pages, 9 illus.
> Blazing our nights with arguments uproarious;
> What care we for a dull old world censorious?
> When each is sure he'll fashion something glorious.   —John Reed

As the new century begins, the Muckrakers, journalists working for social reform, join in creating what writer and editor Max Eastman called "a self-conscious entity, an American Bohemia or Gypsy-minded Latin Quarter." O. Henry's clarion call to writers exemplifies the attraction the Village has for the rest of America.

Walter Lippmann, Theodore Dreiser, Eugene O'Neill, Lincoln Steffens, Willa Cather, John Dos Passos, Floyd Dell, Edward Arlington Robinson, Harry Kemp, and Maxwell Bodenheim pour into the Village and into this chapter.

Many of them live in "The House of Genius," Madame Catherine Branchard's boardinghouse on Washington Square South which, John Reed crooned, "sheltered inglorious Miltons by the score, and Rodins, one to every floor."

Readers meet the Miltons, the Rodins, and the characters: suffragist Henrietta Rodman, the first uncorseted "Village Girl," anarchist Hippolyte Havel, and restaurant owner Polly Holliday.

Backed by the patronage of Gertrude Vanderbilt Whitney, the "Ashcan School" of artists led by John Sloan and Robert Henri protest old-fashioned "pretty pictures." An account of the Armory Show of 1913, which introduced a shocked America to modern art, follows.

Then comes Mabel Dodge's salon, which by providing a forum for the Bohemians, puts the Village on the cultural and political map of the United States. This leads to the 1913 pageant in Madison Square Garden for striking silk workers killed in Paterson. The brainchild of Mabel Dodge and John Reed, the pageant unites all the Villagers.

The next section recounts the history of the Liberal Club, the Village's meeting place, and its voice, *The Masses*, a heady mixture of politics, art, literature, and humor.

Then the curtain rises on the Provincetown Players and its first production, in 1916, of Eugene O'Neill's *Bound East for Cardiff*. Other new theater groups, including the Washington Square Players, also have their moment on the stage in this chapter.

Joyous Bohemia closes with the 1916 sit-in for the Republic of Washington Square on top of Washington Square Arch by John Sloan, Marcel Duchamp, and a melancholy poet named Woe, "because Woe is Me."

Illustrations: Paintings of Village life by Ashcan artists William Glackens and Glenn O. Coleman; photos of Polly's Restaurant, Mabel Dodge's salon, John Reed, the Paterson pageant, and the Provincetown Players; an illustration from *The Masses*; and *The Revolution of Washington Square*, an engraving by John Sloan.

Different Books, Different Challenges

How-to Books

How-to books are staples in the book business. Publishers welcome fresh ideas that offer readers the opportunity to lead better, richer lives. Successful how-tos present a new idea at the right time; or are written by an expert, celebrity, or promotable personality; or if a publisher's lucky, have a strong idea, a strong personality, and the right timing going for them. People want to know, but they don't want to learn, so your challenge is to make it as easy and enjoyable as possible for them.

How-to books use six techniques to present their material:

1. They have a down-to-earth, me-to-you tone.

2. They include anecdotes to create a rapport with readers.

3. They give readers something to do to keep them involved.

4. If they are teaching a new skill, they present it in a systematic way which is reflected in the book's title.

5. They provide the book's benefit simply, clearly, and step by step, teaching readers how to improve themselves or their lives.

6. They supplement the text with accurate, attractive illustrations.

If you are writing an instructional book like an exercise book or a cookbook, start each outline by describing the chapter's introductory remarks and plan on including copy between exercises or recipes. Besides creating a rapport between you and the reader, it allows your personality to shine through, breaks up the instructional material, and makes the book a pleasure to read.

An effective how-to title incorporates the notions of a desirable activity or skill to be learned, a systematic approach to learning it, and if possible, a time within which the reader will acquire the skill. *French Made Simple, 30 Days to Building a Greater Vocabulary, Total Fitness in 30 Minutes a Week* are selling titles.

Biographies

Biographies present a real temptation to summarize instead of outlining. "First, she did this, then she did this, and then she did this, etc." But if your summaries and sample chapters are rich enough, the proposal will still work. Brief passages of dialogue that convey the drama in scenes will enhance the summary.

But the following outline of the first chapter of Randy Shilts's proposal for *The Mayor of Castro Street: The Life & Times of Harvey Milk* shows that it is possible to outline a biography in the outline form recommended above:

Part I: The Years Without Hope
Chapter 1
The Men Without Their Shirts   16 pages
Time: 1930-Korean War

The chapter opens with the story of how police round up a teenage Harvey Milk with other gay men cruising Central Park, marching them off to a paddy wagon for the crime of taking off their shirts in a gay section of Central Park.

The police march the group through a family section of the park where shirtless men are left unmolested. For the first time, Milk realizes there's something wrong in society's treatment of gays.

This opening symbolizes both Milk's life as a homosexual growing up decades before the phrase "gay rights" was ever muttered, and it also indicates the overall social climate facing gays of that era. The chapter develops both of these themes.

On the personal side, this segment outlines Milk's early family life on Long Island and later his college years in Albany. Many of Milk's personality traits are evident during these years: his lust for the limelight, his stubborn dogmatism, his sense of humor, and most significantly, his intense interest in politics.

Milk's ramblings in New York's gay milieu of the mid-forties and fifties offer an opportunity to capsulize the social and political status of gays at that time. The chapter also briefly touches on the homosexual emancipation movement in Germany, which thrived well into the 1920s.

After telling about an experience of four-year-old Harvey Milk, for example, the narrative shifts to Germany in the same year when, on "The Night of the Long Knives," Hitler wiped out Germany's gay subculture. That marked the beginning of the dictator's attempts to exterminate homosexuals.

The gay genocide—coupled with the Jewish holocaust—exerts a powerful influence on Milk's thinking. Through such historical digressions, the first chapter introduces the book's four levels (described earlier).

This chapter ends when Milk, at the apex of a budding career in the Navy, is booted out of the service because of his homosexuality.

Photos: Milk at four on a pony, and in Navy uniform.

Interview Books

Depending upon what you're writing about, books based on interviews can be a problem. If you plan to write the history of Los Angeles in the movies, for instance, the data you need are available. If you outline it well, an editor can easily assess the proposal.

It's harder to predict the value of future interviews, especially if you can't provide an editor a list of interview subjects. Even knowing your interview subjects is no guarantee you'll come away with a book's worth of publishable material. It can also be more difficult to predict the length of your chapters.

Another publishing reality to mull over: Publishers' sales reps travel from Miami to Seattle and they want books of interest to book buyers in their territories. If an idea has national scope, the research for it should be nationwide.

If, for example, you're profiling new-age entrepreneurs, you can't just cover those in your area. Aim for as much diversity in location, background, type of business, experience, attitude, and life-style as you can in those you interview. Editors will expect the book to be comprehensive in presenting the range of the entrepreneurial experience. Include people from major cities (which are also major book markets) and all regions of the country. The regional variations you encounter will add depth to your book.

HOT TIP   *Use the opportunity to travel and meet people to develop a national network of readers, booksellers, and media contacts you can make use of when your book is published.*

Interviews in your area, perhaps supplemented by telephone interviews elsewhere, may suffice for the proposal. You naturally want to minimize your expenses on a proposal that might not sell. But the Overview and outline should indicate that the manuscript will contain interviews from around the country.

A problem might arise later if your interviews don't yield the material you want and you need more time or money to obtain additional interviews. Plan your research carefully and give yourself a cushion.

Interviewing as many people as you can in your initial research will enrich the proposal, teach you how to overcome pitfalls, and provide leads for other interviews. The most convincing argument for an interview book is a hefty portion—a third to a half—of the manuscript.

Writers with interview articles to their credit may be attracted by the notion of doing a book of interviews, thinking to themselves: "Hey, I'll find 20 people who need publicity, do ten 10-page interviews and I'll have me a book." Well, editors aren't wild about collections of anything, including interviews, unless the interviews are wedded by a very salable idea, or are with celebrities or VIPs whom people want to know more about, or the interviewer is famous, or all three.

Editors would much rather you take an idea and develop it for 200 pages, using interview material to prove your points. For them, that's what makes a book a book.

Humor Books

At this writing, the market for humor books is down, and unless you have a track record, humor is hard to sell with a proposal. It's difficult to prove that you can be funny for the length of a book, even a short one. So if you can't deliver all of the manuscript, try to submit at least a third of it to present a solid sampling of your sense of humor. If you're doing a cartoon book with captions, provide all of the captions, as many drawings as possible, and a description of the remaining drawings.

Exposés

Controversy can sell books if it's the right subject at the right time with an author who can publicize the book in a way that catches the attention of the media and the public. *Silent Spring, The American Way of Death, Unsafe at Any Speed, All the President's Men, Indecent Exposure,* and *The Fate of the Earth* have proven it.

Yet in general, people don't like to get depressed, and they sure don't want to pay for the privilege. That's why unless they involve Hollywood, politics, big business, or some other juicy subject with built-in national interest, exposés in general don't sell.

If your book will bring bad news, try to be prescriptive as well as descriptive. People don't want problems, they want solutions. They want to take a book like they take a pill. So develop a program for improving the situation. This will give your book a positive slant which should be reflected in the title and in sales.

When David Armstrong wanted to write an exposé of the health food industry with the title *The Health Food Hustlers,* I suggested that it might be more salable if he called it *The Insider's Guide to Health Foods,* and that's the title Bantam used to publish it. *Claiming Your Share* is an exposé, but Michelle Saadi turned the idea into a public service.

Anthologies

Anthologies also don't light up the cash registers. In the book trade, even the word *anthology* is deadly. Avoid the notion of a collection in the title, if possible. *I'm On My Way Running: Women Speak on Coming of Age* sounds like an anthology, but the title is certainly more appealing without the word.

If you're doing a *treasury* (a less academic, more selling word), start with a strong concept, make sure the selections are worth including, that they measure up well against each other, and that the book will hold up over time.

Selections should also flow easily from one to the next. Splitting up the book into parts and chapters and writing an introduction for each section helps ensure this.

Getting permissions, also covered earlier, can be a time-consuming problem because copyright holders may be abroad, may not respond to your inquiries, may charge you an exorbitant fee, or may refuse to quote a price until they have specific details about the book's publication. Yet it's important that your proposal include as accurate an estimate of permissions costs as you can obtain.

A Final Thought

Your outline is the foundation of your book. A sturdy, cohesive foundation will go far in convincing an editor to back your proposal. A thorough outline may also prevent your book from being rejected. If you deliver your manuscript on time, and it lives up to what your proposal promises, your editor will have no reason to reject it.

How exact a blueprint your outline is for the finished manuscript will depend on how well the outline is done, the need to explore new avenues of investigation, suggestions your editor may make, and how cut-and-dried or open-ended the subject is.

Your book may change unexpectedly because of new ideas or information or an unpredictable turn of events. But properly done, the structure you create for your book should serve you well as a framework for writing a book you can be proud of.

CHAPTER FOUR

The Sample Chapters

At this point in the proposal, the editor knows you have a strong idea and a book's worth of information about it. At least one sample chapter will answer the question: How well can you write the book?

After hooking the editor to the subject and the book, the sample material is the most important part of the proposal. It's the only chance you have to strut your stuff, to prove that you have what it takes to write the book. A humor book must make the editor laugh and a dramatic book must have the impact you want the book to have.

Begin this third section of the proposal with the heading:

Sample Chapters

Chapter X

Title of Chapter

How many chapters you write will depend on the time, energy, information, and other resources at your disposal, as well as how many sample chapters an editor has to see to reach a favorable decision. Since you're working on your own, you want to minimize your time, effort, and expense.

How much of the book should I send an editor?

If you're writing a humorous account of your experiences as a cabdriver, or a dramatic story with mounting suspense about the solution of a crime, or an inspirational book about someone who has overcome formidable obstacles to achieve a goal, as with a novel, the cumulative impact of the material will be stronger if an editor reads the whole manuscript.

For most books, however, editors prefer to see a thorough proposal and 30 to 50 pages of manuscript or two sample chapters.

Remember: The goal of your proposal is to generate the maximum amount of excitement with the minimum number of words. So the criterion for deciding how much more than two chapters to send is: Will an additional chapter create enough additional excitement to justify including it?

When aren't two chapters necessary?

An editor doesn't have to see every exercise or recipe to know if a how-to book is publishable. If your book will be a series of chapters identical in structure and with the same kind of information, such as a travel guide or an exercise book, one sample chapter will suffice. For instance, if you were going to write that guidebook to Europe's ten greatest cities mentioned earlier, an editor will only have to see how you handle one city.

If you have a choice of which chapter to prepare, choose the most exciting one you can write. When you're sending only one chapter, it must be representative. It should come from the heart of the book, a shining example of what is innovative and stimulating about the subject.

What if my book is depressing?

If your subject is depressing, try to make at least part of your sample material upbeat so that, if possible, an editor will finish reading your proposal feeling positive about the subject as well as the proposal.

What if it's a fill-in-the-blank book?

Libraries don't like "fill-in" books because their borrowers fill them in. So if your book will require readers to write exercises or respond to questions, unless it's essential for them to write in the book, ask them to use a piece of paper or a notebook.

Also keep in mind that sample chapters should present a sample of your writing. If your entire book will consist only of a series of fill-ins, perhaps you should submit the whole manuscript or at least a substantial chunk of it.

Should I send the Introduction?

You may not be able to write certain chapters because they require time, travel, or other resources you need an advance to obtain.

You may want to write the introductory chapter, but in a how-to book, for instance, an introduction will not demonstrate how you will treat the instructional material which is the heart of the book. For this reason, writers often do both an introductory chapter and one solid, representative chapter.

For most books, whether or not they will have an introductory chapter, two strong sample chapters will give both you and an editor confidence that you can and want to write about the subject. And as your in-house agent whose job it is to stir up interest in your book, an editor needs that confidence to fight for your book.

If knowing the concepts in your introductory chapter is essential to understanding the outline, insert the introductory chapter at the beginning of the outline, and the other sample material after it.

Do the chapters have to be in sequence?

Sample chapters don't have to be from the beginning of the book or in sequence. But do make your sample material complete segments or chapters, not a part of one or more chapters. An editor will want to see how a complete slice of the book reads.

If, however, you are putting together a collection of some kind, and you can get pieces of every chapter but not a complete chapter, outline each chapter thoroughly, and after each outline, include 10 percent of the material from the chapter. Even if you are providing sample chapters, if you have all of the recipes or exercises for your book, for example, including the best 10 percent of each chapter after each outline will help an editor see the book's strengths.

Which chapters do I send?

If you're not sure which chapters to use as samples, preparing the outline will help you decide. Certain chapters usually stand out as being easier to do and more impressive for an editor to read. Give it your best shot in choosing what to write and in how well you write it.

What if I have finished more of the book than I submit?

You will be mentioning on the resource page how much of the manuscript is finished. If editors want to see more than you submit, they will contact you.

Can I get away with not sending a chapter?

If you've already written a book on the subject, you may not need any sample chapters; an outline, perhaps submitted with the book, may suffice. Another circumstance in which you may not need sample material is if you have had several books published which testify to your ability to write the book you are proposing. Teaching, running a professional practice, or staff or free-lance journalism of high quality over a period of years may also be sufficient to prove your credentials. But if you don't prepare sample material, your outline must be extensive and impeccable.

What if I haven't had anything published?

If you have had no articles or books for the general public published, and the proposal is all an editor will have to go on, you should submit more of the manuscript, a third to a half, depending on how ambitious the project is and how well you write.

What if my book has no chapters?

If your book doesn't break up into chapters, you should still provide an editor with at least 10 percent of the completed manuscript.

If you're proposing a picture book, make the project more substantial by writing a lengthy introduction and providing captions and/or a running text. Unless a large national audience already exists for your work, or your idea is extremely commercial, your book will need more than just illustrations. Unless they're getting your book to give as a gift, or unless they feel they must own it, browsers won't buy your book if they can finish it in the store.

Editors are print people. They want text to explain illustrations. They also want a compelling reason to go to the effort and expense of producing a picture book. As for the illustrations you include in the proposal, they should be gorgeous, and in their diversity, representative of the range of illustrations that will be in the book.

If you can obtain the services of an experienced book designer, include a mechanical, a camera-ready pasteup with type, photos, and line art on art board. Make a page no larger than 8½" x 11" and include two facing pages as an example of your visual approach to the book.

Now you know what editors expect to see in proposals. Once you start doing it, the pieces will start falling into place. The advice that follows will help you give them a nudge.

Illustrations

Illustrations add to a book's salability, but they also make it more expensive and complicated to do both for you and for the publisher. Avoid them unless they're really necessary.

If you plan to use illustrations, the sample chapters should include or account for them. If, for example, the book is about a subject in the news, and it's obvious that photographs are available, you don't have to include samples of them but indicate where photos will appear.

If illustrations play an important role in the book, submit them. When you plan to use an illustration of a person, place, event, or instructional point, indicate this in the text by typing "(Illus. x)" after mentioning what you will illustrate. Number illustrations consecutively. Keep pictures to 8½" x 11" or smaller so they will fit in with the text. If pictures are smaller than 8½" x 11", fasten them on 8½" x 11" sheets.

Each illustration should be on a separate page following the page on which it is mentioned. The illustration page should have the same number as the page of text preceding it followed by the letter a, for example, 27a. If there's more than one picture mentioned on one page of text, go down the alphabet. Underneath the illustration, indicate what number it is and provide an identifying caption.

How you handle captions will depend on your own inclination, the kind of book you're writing, how much explanation your illustrations require, and whether illustrations will be grouped together or spread throughout the book.

One approach that may draw potential readers into the book is to make captions complete enough so that just by looking at the illustrations and reading the captions, browsers can follow the book's development.

If you're sending slides, number them and insert them in plastic sheets that hold 20 slides. Place the slides behind the proposal or in the left pocket of the folder described in the section on how to submit your proposal. Behind them, include a page with numbered captions.

If your book will contain black-and-white photos, use 8" x 10" glossies for the sample chapters. Color illustrations result in heavy production costs for publishers, so unless there's a real need for color, stick to black-and-white, or consider a combination of color and black-and-white. Line drawings are less expensive to produce than photographs, so consider using drawings instead of photographs. Let your preference and comparable books guide you to the right approach to illustrating your book.

Color illustrations may be expensive to duplicate or photocopy for a multiple submission. If the quality of the pictures is less important than their use in illustrating the text, photocopies will suffice. If the illustrations are essential to the effectiveness of the proposal, submit it to just one or a few people at a time, or send just the text and then illustrations when there is an expression of interest. Always send photocopies of artwork and duplicates of slides until an editor requests originals.

If the artwork for your book will be simple, straightforward illustrations subordinate to the text, you may submit rough but neat sketches of them for the sample chapters, and if your publisher won't pay for the final artwork, you can hire an artist after you sell the project.

Illustrations are usually printed in one of three ways: in eight- or 16-page inserts on coated stock for better reproduction, scattered throughout the book on the same stock as the text, or a combination of the two. Gift books are printed entirely on coated stock to enhance the quality of the illustrations and impart a more luxurious feeling to the book. If it's not clear from the proposal how the illustrations should be grouped and you have strong feelings about it, describe how you see them being presented in the Overview.

Sample Clips

Outstanding samples of your published work demonstrate acceptance of your work by publications willing to pay for it and the implicit acceptance of their readers. These are your medals, sample clips that you can brag about. Besides proving that you are a professional, they show editors what you can do.

If you have clips that will impress an editor because of their quality, length, relevance, range of subjects, or the periodicals in which they appeared, include up to six of them. If it's a magazine piece, staple the cover to the neatly clipped article. Originals are more attractive than photocopies, but if you can't afford to lose the originals, top-quality photocopies are okay.

Only send a published book if it will help sell the book you're proposing. Otherwise, wait until an editor asks to see it.

If you don't have a book or clips to include, your proposal is all an editor will have to go on, so the weaker your writing experience, the more compelling your proposal has to be to compensate for it.

HOT TIP *Editors aren't impressed by small or poorly produced periodicals, which are often where a writer's early work appears. Like everything else in the proposal, the clips you submit must be of the highest quality. Use your judgment, but when in doubt, leave it out.*

Cover Art: Putting on a Good Front

Effective cover art can help sell your proposal by giving an editor a feeling for the book and its marketability. But creating cover art is an art unto itself. A paperback cover or a hardcover jacket must be attractive, but it must also sell the book.

If you are an artist or a photographer, or are in advertising, and have a selling title and cover idea—perhaps an illustration from the book—try your hand at it. *But remember that the concept and the execution of the art and type must be of professional quality or it may do more harm than good.* Try out the preliminary sketch and the finished artwork on booksellers and other knowledgeable book people before submitting it. As with your sample clips, when in doubt. . . .

Make the artwork the size of the book you envision but no larger than 8½" x 11" so it fits as the first page of the proposal. If you are planning a multiple submission, consider how well the artwork will copy.

Matters of Form

Here is a suggestion on how to prepare the title page and the table of contents, both of which should be typed double-spaced in upper and lower case letters.

The Title Page

The first page of your proposal will be the title page. About a third of the way down the page along the left margin or in the center of the page, type:

`A Proposal for`

`Title` (either underlined or in italics)

`Subtitle` (either underlined or in italics)

`by` (guess who?); include your degree or your position and affiliation if relevant and impressive, for example:

`Professor of Psychology, Stanford University`

If necessary, add the following two lines:

`Introduction by X`

`First in a Series of X Books on (about) X`

Near the bottom of the page, flush left, type:

`Your street address`

`City, state, ZIP code`

`Area code and day and evening phone numbers`

The Table of Contents

The page after the title page is the table of contents. Besides showing an editor what's ahead, a contents page makes the proposal look carefully organized, like a miniature version of the book it aspires to be. In a long proposal, it will also help editors refer back to particular parts.

List the three parts of the proposal flush left, then indent the sections of each part. At the right margin indicate the page on which each begins:

[Give the title of a book or list the titles of articles and the periodicals in which they appeared.]

Supporting Documents

    Enclosed separately in the folder.

If you find stories in major periodicals, such as a cover story in *Newsweek,* that make your proposal more salable, underline the relevant parts neatly and include them.

If you have more than one story about yourself or rave reviews about a previous book, underline the key points and put the material in the folder separately.

A Word About Words

Readers buy nonfiction for information, not style. But even though knowledge is more important than style, every editor who cares about good books—and that's why editors become editors—is a sucker for fine writing. You want an editor to read your proposal without stopping and with a crescendo of enthusiasm.

Craft leaps off the page instantly. Since editors and agents reject over 90 percent of the proposals and manuscripts they see, they will be delighted if after reading your first paragraph, they can say to themselves: "My God! This one can really write!"

And although style is more important in a biography than in a how-to book, the more pleasurable any book is to read, the better its reviews and the more word-of-mouth recommendations it sparks.

How you write must be as important as what you write; style must be as important as content. If you are serious about being a writer, aim to make your writing as lucid, flowing, creative, brilliant, moving, engaging, entertaining, passionate—in a word, irresistible—as you want your reviews to be.

The indispensable guide to the prose of pros is William Strunk, Jr., and E.B. White's *The Elements of Style*. It inspires as it teaches, by example. The relative calm before starting your proposal is a propitious moment to summon your muse by (re)reading it.

Memorize its 32 golden nuggets on composition and style or put them up on the wall where you write. If something's amiss with your writing, and it's not on that list, it may be covered in the pages that follow.

This advice is based on the problems we have encountered in more than a decade of agenting. Not all of it will apply to you as a writer or to your book. Listen to your muse.

The Spice of Life

Your writing must inspire readers to keep going. For this reason, avoid:

- long words: Keep them simple but don't hesitate if a long word is the best one to use.
- long sentences: Long or complex sentence structures slow the eye. But don't go to the other extreme: avoid sentence fragments.
- long paragraphs: The mind revolts when confronted with unbroken, page-long blocks of copy; aim for three or four paragraphs a page and avoid paragraphs longer than half a page.

However, variety is an essential virtue in prose. An endless succession of short words, sentences, and paragraphs will read like ad copy or a formula approach to writing. The art of writing is the ability to express and structure your ideas so that, regardless of length, every word counts. Stick with the literary standards set by comparable books you admire.

Between the Overview, outline, and sample chapters, an editor may read the same material three times. If there is no way to avoid repeating yourself, vary the wording.

Assume the editor knows only what the average American knows about the subject; terms, concepts, and explanations must be clear.

Avoid cuteness and gratuitous humor.

Filter images of all the senses—sight, sound, touch, taste, and smell—through the reader's imagination to bring to life the people, places, and events you describe. Let the accumulation of details make what you write about convincing. Reality is what you make readers believe.

Like an anecdote, dialogue is action. It breaks up the narrative and enlivens your prose as it develops the story, characters, and atmosphere.

A Cure for Hiccoughs

Using an unusual word, sentence structure, or punctuation, then using it again, and then, since it comes to mind quickly, using it again, is a nasty habit that unwary writers are prey to. The repetition makes it stand out like a writing tic, a literary hiccough.

Given the richness of the language, this suggests either a lack of writing skill or an unwillingness to find the most felicitous way to express a thought. If you start to lapse into the repetition of a word, sentence structure, or punctuation, limit yourself to using the culprit only once every 20 or 30 pages. It's an easier cure for hiccoughs than drinking a glass of water with your head upside down.

If you use two or more nouns or verbs together, make sure that all of them fit the rest of the sentence. I managed to provide an example of this in my manuscript: "For a more professional look, greater protection, and the possibility of resubmitting the proposal elsewhere, insert it. . . ." The word *possibility* does not work well with the preposition *for*. You will see how I revised it in the section on how to submit your proposal.

If you're not sure how well a passage reads, read it aloud. But don't write like you talk unless you're writing dialogue or want to create the effect of speech. When speaking, we take liberties with words and grammar that are acceptable, but come across as improvised, rather than carefully written, when they appear on paper.

Words to Avoid

Avoid the verb *to be* if you can find a stronger verb.

Avoid indefinite words like *maybe, probably, perhaps, few, many, lots of, plenty of, little,* and *several.* Be definite and specific.

Avoid weak verbs. Use *can* for *could; will* for *would, might,* or *should; is* for *seems to be.* Readers want to be informed by an authority, so write like one! The more forceful your statements the better, particularly in the Overview, when you're trying to sell your idea to an editor. Don't pussyfoot around. Be accurate, but be bold.

Avoid negative words or expressions. As *The Elements of Style* says: "Put statements in positive form."

Avoid sexist words or phrasing: use *they* for *he, humanity* for *man* or *mankind.*

Avoid countercultural coinages such as *laid back* or *mellow out.*

Avoid trendy words like *mode, process, viable,* and *parameter.*

Avoid writing *three years ago* or *three years from now;* this may date your proposal. Write *in 1982* or *by 1988.*

Avoid jargon. You may be a psychologist or a computer hacker but not all of your readers are. Don't make your vocabulary a barrier to communication.

Avoid exaggeration.

Avoid superlatives unless they are warranted.

Avoid all-encompassing words like *all, every,* or *never,* unless they are accurate.

Avoid creating new words or bulky word combinations united by hyphens or slash marks. Don't take liberties with the language; it's a glorious instrument which already has enough keys to create all of the color, texture, vitality, variety, and emotion any composition could want.

Avoid inevitable words. If you're writing a book about sex, avoid the word. It's going to show up often enough anyway when there's no alternative. Use a synonym, write around it, or just leave it out. Readers know what you're talking about.

Avoid clichés. Don't use expressions you are used to hearing or seeing in print; be original.

Avoid ordinary, overworked, lifeless words, phrases, and images. Strive to make your writing vivid and colorful. This doesn't mean that you should never use warhorses like *show, tell, make, give, do, good, very, interesting,* and *fascinating.* It means that you should infuse your prose with as much feeling, resonance, and vitality as the subject allows.

Avoid *etc.* You will slow editors down by forcing them to think about what it refers to. Either include the whole list or use part of the list and preface it with *like* or *such as.*

Avoid abbreviations such as *i.e.* and *e.g.* unless, like P.M., they are accepted in formal prose.

Unless standard usage prescribes capital letters, avoid putting words in capital letters for emphasis; it looks amateurish. Let your choice of words and how you position them create the desired effect.

Numbers

If you're writing a how-to book in which numbers are important, such as this one, use words for the numbers 1 to 10 and for numbers at the beginning of sentences. Otherwise, use digits. For other kinds of books, follow the usage in comparable books.

Don't mention cents or the lack of them—.00—when discussing money. Stick to round dollar figures.

Punctuation and Italics

Avoid underlining for emphasis. Underline the names of books and periodicals unless your computer's printer can print them in italics.

Avoid exclamation points; unless really needed, they look like you're trying to force an emotion out of the reader.

As *The Elements of Style* recommends, place a comma after every part of a list except the last.

Avoid parentheses in the Overview and outline. If something's worth saying, say it; if not, leave it out.

Remember to hyphenate a group of words used to modify a noun, when the hyphenation clarifies the meaning. Examples are black-and-white photos, 15-page document, and high-quality work. However, it is no longer considered correct to hyphenate an adjective and an adverb ending in *ly,* as in "beautifully written."

Use quote marks if you're quoting someone and always make it clear whom you're quoting and why. Otherwise, avoid them.

If you use a dash to set off a word or phrase, type two hyphens. No space is necessary between dashes and what surrounds them.

Use a single quote mark as an apostrophe or for a quote within a quote.

Less is More

Think of writing as having two stages: writing for fact and writing for impact. First you have to get the material down on paper and then gradually massage it into final form. Fine writing stands out because of its lack of faults, because authors have the taste to know when a word, sentence, or idea doesn't feel right, and the perseverance to revise their work until it does. A writer at one of my workshops once said her best friend was her wastebasket.

First-time authors may find it difficult to believe, but when it comes to prose, less is more. Good writing is simple, not unnecessarily flashy; direct, not flowery; and concise. Your proposal should tell editors everything you want them to know but in *as few words as possible*. Say what must be said, then move on.

At its best, writing also has passion, vision, and vigor. Editor Toni Burbank once remarked about a manuscript: "There was nothing wrong with it, but there was nothing right with it either." Author Cyra McFadden once lamented about another failed effort: "The prose just lay there, dead on the page." Make your writing live for an editor, who should be your toughest yet most sympathetic critic, and if you have a salable idea, your proposal will sell.

Two More Steps to a 100% Proposal

To submit anything to an agent or publisher before it's 100 percent, as well conceived and well written as you can make it, is a mistake. Don't send drafts and don't send the proposal in pieces. Wait until it's ready.

Once you have written your proposal as well as you can, it's time to find out if you're right. Here are the last two steps to take to make sure that your proposal is 100 percent before you submit it:

1. Let other people read your proposal.

By the time you've finished your proposal, you will need a respite. You may find yourself developing tunnel vision which impairs your ability to judge your work objectively. You may be so close to it that you can't distinguish its faults from its virtues. If you revise a passage often enough, you know it so well that you start to see what's not there. Now's the time to give yourself a break and share your proposal with readers who can advise you on how to improve it.

If you need a pat on the back, let your friends and family read your proposal. They will tell you they like it because they like you. After all, what are friends and family for? If you want sound advice, try these readers:
• potential buyers of the book. They may not know good writing, but they know what they like. Would they buy your book if they found it in a bookstore? See if you can get a bookseller to render an opinion.

- literate, objective readers who can tell you what's wrong with your proposal as well as what's right with it
- experts in the field you are writing about
- readers who disagree with you if you're presenting a controversial idea. Find members of the opposition to go over your proposal and try to poke holes in it. You may not convert them but you might earn their respect and avoid embarrassing yourself later.
- and most valuable of all, the most critical critic, a devil's advocate. A devil's advocate is someone whose literary taste and judgment you respect and in whose knowledge of books and writing you have absolute confidence. A devil's advocate can combine truth with charity and while analyzing the overall vision and development of the book, can spot every word, punctuation mark, sentence structure, idea, character, and incident that can be improved or removed. Devil's advocates are worth their weight in royalties.

See if you can get one or more of these angels to read these instructions before reading your proposal so they can judge if it covers all the bases.

To find the readers you need for your work, build a network of people in and out of the publishing world who are interested in your work: objective friends and relatives if you are lucky enough to have them, omnivorous readers, teachers, writers, librarians, booksellers, reviewers, whomever you can corral to pay attention to your work.

Since people like to see their names in print, maybe you can bribe reluctant readers by promising them that you will mention them on the acknowledgments page. You can also promise them autographed copies.

The Hired Pen

If nobody else is available, consider hiring a freelance editor who has worked on proposals and on published nonfiction books for the general public. At this writing, freelance editors charge $10-$25 an hour, so the editing of a 70-page proposal might cost $1,000.

When you find an editor you want to work with, ask him or her to read this guide to understand what you want to write. Then get an assessment of the proposal and an estimate of what it will cost to edit it and a revision based on the editor's recommendations. Check the listings in *Literary Market Place* if your writing network doesn't lead you to any editors in your area.

2. Integrate changes into a final revision.

Since reactions are subjective, receiving more than one may prepare you for the varying responses your book may arouse. You may have to sift conflicting and even confusing suggestions and follow the advice that makes the most sense to you. Trust your instincts.

Once you have sorted out the opinions of others and feel ready to return to your proposal with a fresh eye, go over it again and do a final revision. When you're sure your proposal is ready, it's time to send your baby out into the real world.

CHAPTER FIVE

How to Submit
Your Proposal

The appearance of your proposal reflects the professionalism with which you are approaching the agent or editor, the subject, and your career. It's the tangible evidence of the care you will lavish on the book. Consequently, the impression of you it makes affects readers' reactions to the proposal.

Make your proposal a document that looks like it's worth the advance you want for it. Agents and editors know from experience that there is usually a relationship between how writers submit manuscripts and how they write them.

Type your proposal immaculately on one side of 8½"x11" 20-pound bond paper. Never use slippery erasable paper or onionskin. Type everything, including quotes and anecdotes, double-spaced. Avoid "widows," a subhead at the bottom of a page or the last line of a chapter at the top.

HOT TIP   *If you want your proposal to stand out, instead of using regular bond paper, use a higher quality, textured stock. It will make your proposal look like a class act.*

Your typewriter should have standard, serif, pica (10 characters to an inch) type, a new ribbon, and clean keys. If you have a word processor, use a letter-quality printer. Don't justify the right margin; leave that for the typesetter.

Type 25 60-character lines, about 250 words, on a page. Set 1¼" margins on the top and sides of the page (1¾" if you must use an elite typewriter).

Type your name, address, and day and evening phone numbers on the title page.

At the left margin of each page, half an inch from the top, type your last name and first key word from the title separated by a slash mark. On the same line, flush right, type the number of the page:

Number pages consecutively from 1 to the end of the proposal, not by section or chapter, so that if your proposal is dropped, it will be easy to put the pages back in order.

Proofread your proposal carefully and get an eagle-eyed friend to check your work. If you're using a computer, proofread a printout to catch what you may have missed on the screen, especially those extra spaces between words that can sneak in when you revise.

Always submit material unbound, without staples or any form of binding. Paper clips are acceptable, but they leave indentations on the paper. Send a high-quality photocopy of your text and illustrations, or duplicates of slides.

For a more professional look, and greater protection in case you have to resubmit the proposal, insert it in the right side of a colored, double-pocket construction-paper portfolio. You can use the left pocket for writing samples, illustrations, and supporting documents. Put a self-adhesive label on the front of the folder with the title and your name.

Where to Submit Your Proposal

In *Megatrends*, John Naisbitt writes that America is evolving from an either/or society to a multiple-option society. This is already true when it comes to getting your book published.

You can self-publish it, which, because of the growth of personal computers and short-run printing, more and more writers are doing.

You can package it.

You can pay part of the publishing costs to a subsidy publisher or all of the publishing costs to a vanity publisher.

Your book could be published by a small or large house, a regional or national one, a scholarly or university press, or a religious publisher.

The choice you make depends on your literary and financial goals and how involved you want to get with the publishing process.

If you want a publisher to put out your book, then once your proposal is ready to mail, the next challenge is to find the right house for it. You have two choices: do it yourself or find an agent.

Finding a Publisher

If you want to find a publisher yourself, the research you have done on competing and complementary books and their publishers will come in handy. Following are six suggestions that will also help you:

1. Publishers Weekly

Either subscribe to *Publishers Weekly* or read it at the library, but keep track of which publishers are doing books on your subject. The spring and fall announcement issues will be particularly helpful.

2. Bookstores

Haunt bookstores, keep track of the books that are coming out in your field, talk to booksellers, and develop a sense of which publishers turn out good books and promote them well.

HOT TIP *"Cluster publishing" is one of the realities of the book world. Publishers develop a knack and a reputation for doing certain kinds of books well—gimmick books, serious nonfiction, beauty books, books about wine, sports, or new-age subjects. At large houses, usually one or more editors will specialize in particular subjects. You may be able to find out who does what with a phone call to the editor-in-chief's assistant.*

The other side of this coin is that houses may be reluctant to publish in a field in which they've had no experience and will probably avoid a book if they've had a bad experience with a similar book.

---

3. The publishing community

Talk to your professional network of writers, writers' groups, editors, writing teachers, booksellers, librarians, reviewers, publicists, and publishers' sales representatives. Ask them which publishers would be right for your book.

4. Directories

Literary Market Place (LMP), which is in your library, is the annual directory of the publishing industry. It lists publishers and their fields of interest. *Writer's Market*, an annual sold in bookstores, also lists publishers, and since it is published for writers, it goes into more detail about publishers' needs and requirements.

5. Magazines

Writer's Digest and *The Writer* do annual publisher roundups.

6. Books

For names of specific editors, check the acknowledgments pages of books similar to yours.

Following up on these suggestions will generate a list of possible publishers for you to query. You may be able to query editors at small houses by phone.

The nature of your book will determine how many alternatives you have in choosing a publisher. If it's a guidebook to Seattle, you'd better look for a publisher who specializes in regional books. If it's a book about karate, you may need to find a publisher who does martial-arts books. If it's a rather narrow subject such as a biography of a lesser-known writer, it might be right for a small alternative or academic press. University presses generally publish books by scholars for scholars, so you need impressive credentials and a subject with academic interest to be published by them.

Because large houses have high overheads and need books that can help maintain them, if your book will interest only a small number of book buyers, consider trying small houses, which have smaller monthly overheads to meet and might be more open-minded and adventurous about the projects they take on.

If your book will have a large national audience, major houses will be glad to hear from you.

Size isn't the only factor in choosing a publisher. Editors have their own tastes, publishers their own character. They do certain kinds of books better than others and have developed widely varying standards for how literary, commercial, serious, practical, well illustrated, and well written they expect their books to be.

Look in the announcement issues of *Publishers Weekly*, get publishers' catalogs, and talk to book people about the houses you are considering to help you decide which houses might be right for your book and which ones you will be comfortable working with.

Trade-offs

Large houses have the resources to provide bigger advances and better promotion and distribution than small houses. Their books receive more attention from booksellers, reviewers, and sub rights buyers. But a small book can get lost on a large list, communications within large houses may not be good, and you and your book may not get all the attention you would like.

Small houses can't afford to make many mistakes. They really want every book to count. But they have to sell fewer copies to break even and are more likely to succumb to their passion for a book, regardless of how commercial it may be.

Writers usually enjoy a more personal involvement with the editing and production of their books at a small house. Fewer people are involved in the process, and, since you may be dealing with people who own the business, they tend to be committed to what they're doing. They pay less money up front and you'll probably make less in the long run, but your personal involvement and psychic rewards may be greater.

The number of publishers is growing every year, so if you have a salable property, there are more buyers for it out there all the time.

Finding an Agent

Since you can't really tell a publisher's virtues from its size, its location, or its books, and you are after the best possible editor, publisher, and deal for your book, you may want to find a literary agent.

Here are five suggestions for finding an agent:

1. Your Publishing Network

It works for finding an agent as well as a publisher. Ask writers you know or admire for recommendations. Try writers' groups, editors, writing teachers, booksellers, librarians, reviewers, publishers' sales reps, and publicists.

2. SAR and ILAA

The Society of Author's Representatives (SAR) and the Independent Literary Agents Association (ILAA) are the two groups of agents whose members are experienced and reputable.

The SAR was founded in 1928, and its 55 members are for the most part the larger, older agencies. Only New York agents may join. For a brochure and membership list, send a self-addressed stamped envelope (SASE) to SAR, Box 650, Old Chelsea Station, New York, NY 10113.

Formed in 1977 with our agency as one of its charter members, ILAA has about 70 members from generally smaller, newer agencies in and out of New York. For a brochure and membership list, send a SASE to ILAA, 55 Fifth Avenue, New York, NY 10003.

3. Directories

LMP and *Writer's Market* list agents.

Literary Agents: A Writer's Guide, by Debby Mayer, a Poets & Writers Book, contains a listing of agents preceded by an explanation of how agents work and how to find one.

The most comprehensive listing of agents is in *Literary Agents of North America* published by Arthur Orrmont, Author Aid/Research Associates International, 340 East 52nd Street, New York, NY 10022, (212)758-4213. *LANA* lists more than 650 agents in 31 states and Canada, along with their interests and financial arrangements.

4. Literary Events

Writing classes, seminars, and conferences present opportunities to meet or learn about agents.

5. Books

Writers sometimes thank their agents in print, so check acknowledgments pages.

If your proposal is good enough, anybody can sell it because any likely publisher will buy it. Whether you try to sell it yourself or enlist the help of a literary agent, the goal is to get your proposal into the hands of the right editor at the right house at the right time.

If you market your book yourself, send it to as many competent, reputable publishers as you can find. Depending upon the audience for your book, that could be five or 50. If none of them takes it, go on to your next project. And as Jane Adams, author of *How to Sell What You Write* (Putnam, 1984) advises, don't regard unsold work as a loss, look at it as inventory which one day will sell.

Your book is your baby. If you submit it to an irresponsible editor or publisher, or a house that will bury it instead of publish it, your book will become a source of grief instead of parental pride.

Since more agents and publishers dot the landscape all the time, it is getting increasingly easier to find a home for a salable book.

If your proposal is accepted, allow a month for the contract to arrive and another month for the advance. The actual time will depend on the size and efficiency of the house, what else is going on in the house at the time, and how complicated the deal is.

The Cover Letter

Once you've queried agents or editors, they will be expecting your proposal, so your covering letter doesn't have to be elaborate. Keep it to one page of single-spaced copy. Start by reminding them that you're sending your proposal because they expressed interest in it.

Then in two or three paragraphs, describe the essence of your book, the markets for it, and your background. Try to avoid repeating the proposal or diminishing its impact.

If you want to do a multiple submission, specify in your covering letter that other editors are looking at the proposal. If you want to do a multiple submission to agents, ask them first.

Photocopies of your proposal are fine, but use originals for your covering letter. Always include your address and phone numbers in your correspondence.

Proper Packaging

Someone once defined a manuscript as "something submitted in haste and returned at leisure." For the best treatment at the receiving end, submit your proposal properly.

As agents and publishers do not assume responsibility for lost or damaged manuscripts, it behooves you to package your proposal carefully. Place the proposal in a manila envelope or, for greater protection, a #5 mailing bag.

In his book *How to Write Short Stories*, Ring Lardner warned: "A good many young writers make the mistake of enclosing a stamped, self-addressed envelope, big enough for the manuscript to come back in. This is too much of a temptation to the editor." Lardner may have a point there, but agents and editors have no obligation to return submissions unless you provide them with the means to do so.

Always enclose a stamped, self-addressed mailer if you want the material returned. If you don't need the material back, say so. But include a stamped, self-addressed #10 envelope for a response. Five staples will seal a mailing bag effectively; avoid string or tape.

Naturally you want to be sure your proposal arrives. However, *don't call!* Agents and editors dislike wasting their time with did-you-get-it? calls. Use United Parcel Service, spring for a return receipt at the post office, or enclose a postcard with your address filled in and the following message on the back:

```
We received (Title) on _____.

We will get back to you by _____.

Name _____.

Title _____.
```

If you don't use a postcard, find out by phone or by mail how long the reading will take before you send your proposal, and if you haven't heard by then, call or write to find out when you can expect a response. A six-to-eight-week turnaround is typical for agents, and publishers vary in how quickly they process submissions.

The View from the 23rd Floor

Where you stand depends on where you sit.

—Miles's Law

Imagine for a moment that you are the harried editor on the 23rd floor of a midtown Manhattan monolith who is about to read your proposal. As an editor, you know that even completed manuscripts are a gamble because unless a book is written by a best-selling author or a celebrity or has an irresistibly commercial idea behind it, it is impossible to predict how reviewers and book buyers will react to it.

A proposal adds another element of risk because as an editor at a major house who's been around for a while, you have seen thousands of proposals and have been burned by your share of them that:

• never resulted in completed manuscripts because the author ran out of steam or couldn't write the book.

• developed ideas that ultimately didn't have enough depth for a book.

• turned into outstanding manuscripts that arrived too late to publish, sometimes because a writer gave another project higher priority.

• led to published books that reached the stores when interest in the subject had been satisfied, veered in another direction, or simply dried up.

• got no reviews and didn't sell.

• got bad reviews and didn't sell.

• got rave reviews but didn't sell anyway.

If the proposal is for a first book, then as an editor, you have more reason for uncertainty, because it is impossible to prove that the writer can turn out a publishable manuscript.

At the same time, part of your job and one of your joys as an editor is discovering new talent. But since the average investment your house makes in a book is more than $40,000, the high cost of failure forces you to minimize risks. You have come to the point as an editor where it's important for the books you acquire to show a profit, if for no other reason than that you want to keep your job.

As a writer, you are now aware of the resistance awaiting your proposal. The directions in these pages will help you overcome that resistance.

It may take one day or five years to sell your proposal. It may sell after a successful book creates an audience for your work. It may never sell because the idea or the proposal isn't as strong as you think it is, or it's ahead of its time, or too late, or for other reasons such as the state of the economy, which have nothing to do with the quality of your proposal.

THE HOTTEST TIP OF ALL *This book could help change your life. If you have a salable idea, prepare a proposal, and sell it, you will no longer be just a writer with an idea. You will be an author with a book to your credit. You will have increased your writing skills, your understanding of publishing and promotion, and the number of professional contacts you know who can help you. All of these strengths will make you more valuable to your publisher because you will be a better writer and more able to help make your books successful.*

As an author, you will be in a position to go from book to book and advance to advance, as long as you, your agent, or your editor can come up with book ideas and you can write proposals and books based on them.

To sustain your momentum, however, you must keep turning ideas into proposals. Unless you plan to continue researching your book while your completed proposal is being sold, go on to your next proposal immediately. Unless you need breathing room between books, aim to have the check for your next advance arrive as soon as your editor accepts the manuscript for the previous book.

So once you or your agent start submitting your proposal, unless you need time to recharge your batteries, continue researching your book or start your next proposal. Since the proposal may not sell, don't waste time waiting for it to happen. You are also less likely to suffer "postpartum depression" after your baby leaves the nest if you have another project to jump into.

No matter how experienced a writer you are, a fantastic idea may hit you at any time. Be ready to take advantage of it!

The Last Word

Every book is a book, yet every book is different, a unique combination of content, author, publisher, and timing. There is no one way to write a proposal any more than there is one way to write a book. Once you hit the keys, you must rely on your common sense and trust your instincts.

We believe that, however arduous this approach may be, it's the fastest, easiest way to get the best possible editor, publisher, and deal for your book, and for creating the best possible book. Ignoring even part of it may cost you time, money, or both.

Even if an editor likes your idea and your style, a weak proposal will force the editor to request a meatier version, dampening at least temporarily the editor's eagerness, slowing the project's momentum, delaying the sale, and making work for you. It's better to do it right the first time than risk not being able to overcome an editor's first and perhaps lasting impression of the project.

I guarantee that if you have a salable idea and it is properly presented to the right editor at the right publishing house at the right time, you will sell it. Good luck!

Appendix

We chose the following proposal by Charles Rubin as a sample because of its brevity and its excellence. It does exactly what a proposal is supposed to do: sell the book and the author in as few words as possible. If a publisher wanted a book on how to buy portable computers (and Addison-Wesley did), the editor would have to say yes to this proposal; it gives an editor no reason to say no. Because of Charles's expertise in the field, he did not have to write a sample chapter.

A Proposal for

Thinking Small

The Buyer's Guide to Portable Computers

by Charles A. Rubin

Rubin/Thinking   1

Introduction

<u>Overview</u>

    In May 1981, the Osborne 1 portable computer was introduced
at the West Coast Computer Fair in San Francisco. Within two
weeks, there was a three-month backlog of orders for this new
computer, and by the end of that year some 40,000 Osbornes had
been sold to a public eager for a product that made computing
power truly mobile.

    This new concept of portable computing fired the popular
imagination and generated countless new computer applications,
and with them new computer users. Managers, salespeople,
journalists, lawyers, and other professionals could take their
offices with them wherever they went; farmers, oil drillers,
archaeologists, and others whose remote locations had kept them
out of the desktop computing revolution could now take part in
it; and students could easily move the new computer between
classroom, library, and dormitory room. If the personal computer
revolution of the mid to late 70's made computing power possible
for everyone, the portable computer revolution of 1981 made it
accessible to anyone, anywhere.

    The overnight success of the Osborne 1 wasn't lost on the
rest of the microcomputer industry. Soon half a dozen companies
were selling portables as the customer base expanded and the
revolution continued. Technological advances like bubble memory

Rubin/Thinking   2

and LCD displays were quickly incorporated into smaller, lighter computers. Industry giants like Commodore, Epson, Radio Shack, NEC, Sharp, and Toshiba brought out their own portable computers one by one until today over three dozen such products are available, with new ones appearing regularly. The variety of features, applications, and price ranges is unmatched by any other segment of the microcomputer industry as new products generate new applications, and new applications broaden the user base, and new users demand new products in a dizzying cycle. New portable computers are front-page news in a dozen computer magazines, but with the ever-widening array of products, features, and technologies assaulting them, would-be portable buyers are often at a loss as to where to begin their search.

Thinking Small: The Buyer's Guide to Portable Computers will be the first book to steer consumers through the current jungle of portable computers, sorting out the prices, features, and applications of every portable computer on the market and offering a step-by-step evaluation and buying guide that will cover over 50 software products, 30 suitcase-sized portable computers, 4 briefcase computers, and 5 notebook computers. The book will contain 191 pages, 41 photos and illustrations, and an index. Written in a conversational, yet economical style, the book will be accessible to computer novices without being too simple-minded for experienced users.

For the novices, the book will offer clear descriptions of a basic microcomputer system, and will explain how portable

computers differ from desktop models. First-time buyers will

also benefit from the book's four-step buying method, which comes

complete with a needs analysis chart to help them find the

portable that's right for them. For users of all levels, the

book will offer a complete listing of portable computer hardware

and software that includes prices, features, history, reputation,

and evaluations of each product in relation to portability

(criteria such as case integrity and battery life). Photographs

of computers will enhance readers' understanding.

Potential markets for this book are as varied as the

computer book market itself, which is making publishing history

because of its growth rate. With their bundled software and ease

of setup, full-featured portables are often serious contenders as

the product of choice for first-time computer buyers. At the

same time, owners of desktop computers are increasingly buying

second computers, and they are more than likely to choose a

portable in order to leverage their computing power.

The book can be marketed in retail bookstores, computer

stores (some of which now specialize in portable computers),

software stores, as well as through book clubs like the Quality

Paperback Book Club (which recently offered Peter McWilliams' The

Word Processing Book as an alternate selection).

When new portable computers appear, the book's appeal can be

maintained through subsequent editions that include the latest

Rubin/Thinking   4

hardware and software. Through my position as an associate

editor of <u>Personal</u> <u>Computing</u> magazine, I often have access to new

computers months before they're commercially available, which

will help make each edition as timely as possible.

The back matter will include a one-page bibliography and an

index.

Rubin/Thinking   5

Resources Needed to Complete the Book

Travel: Boston--3 days

White Plains--2 days

Newark--8 days

Philadelphia--2 days

Fort Lauderdale--2 days

Chicago--2 days

Detroit--2 days

Cincinnati--2 days

Fort Worth--4 days

Houston--2 days

Los Angeles--5 days

Corvallis--2 days

Boulder--2 days

TOTAL: 13 cities--38 days

Photos: 1 staged photo (Chapter 1): $100

Graphics: 2 charts (Chapter 5): $150

2 drawings (Chapter 8): $200

The manuscript will be finished nine months after receipt of the advance.

Rubin/Thinking   6

About the Author

Charles Rubin is currently working as an associate editor of
Personal Computing magazine, where his feature articles appear
monthly. Recent computer subjects he has covered include
portable computers (May issue), computerized farms management
(June issue), computer inventory control (July issue), and
computerphobia (August issue). In addition, he writes software
reviews for Hayden Publishing's new magazine, Personal Software,
which will debut in September 1983. A follower of the personal
computer industry for years, he currently owns two computers and
free-lances computer-related features to other publications. One
feature on hand-held computers will appear in the June 12 edition
of the San Jose Mercury-News.

His other publication credits include a monthly column and
feature articles about San Francisco history for Pacific magazine,
feature articles about agriculture and international trade for
the 1982 Los Angeles Chamber of Commerce International Tradebook,
news features for the Media Alliance's monthly newspaper Media
File, radio advertisements for Pacific magazine, and editing
responsibilities for three corporate newsletters as well as
various small-business brochures and sales letters. He was also
a cofounder and editor of San Francisco Stories, a two-volume
review of contemporary short fiction published in 1980-81; and
was the principal author and researcher of Cable Car Legacy, a
history of San Francisco cable cars intended as a supplement for

Rubin/Thinking 7

the Campaign to Save the Cable Cars.

Charles received his B.A. (magna cum laude) and M.A. degrees from San Francisco State University in 1978 and 1980. He was Creative Writing Student of the Year in 1978 and was an associate editor of the English department's literary magazine, Alchemy. He currently lives in Vallejo, California, with his wife and son.

Rubin/Thinking   8

Chapter-by-Chapter Outline

PART I: GETTING ACQUAINTED

Chapter 1

About This Book   8 pages, 1 photo

The chapter begins with a brief history of portable computers from May 1981 (when the Osborne 1 computer was introduced) to the present time. It describes the four basic reasons for the Osborne's instant success: (1) bundled software, (2) unintimidating size and ease of setup, (3) low price, and (4) portability.

The chapter goes on to describe early products that sought to compete directly with the Osborne, later products that were positioned above the Osborne (and offered at a higher price), and products reflecting newer technologies such as bubble memory, LCD displays, microfloppy disk drives, and long-lasting, quick-charging internal batteries.

The chapter closes by pointing out that some three dozen portable computers are now fighting fiercely for consumer dollars and that this guide is an effort to arm consumers with the information they need to make informed buying decisions. Chapter 1 is set off from Chapter 2 by a photo showing several makes of portable computers in a group shot.

Rubin/Thinking   9

Chapter 2

Computer Basics

Elements of a Computer System   18 pages, 4 photos

The chapter starts by describing the elements of a basic
computer system: the central processing unit (CPU); the internal
memories: random access memory (RAM) and read only memory (ROM);
the operating system; the software; the keyboard; the display;
mass storage (disk drives); interfaces; and the printout device.

The Portable Difference

Using these elements, the section continues with a presentation of the differences and similarities between desktop computers and portable computers.

The Differences Among Portables

At this point the chapter explains that portable computers
fall into three categories: suitcase-sized, briefcase, and
notebook, the differences being that suitcase-sized portables
attempt to offer keyboard, processor, storage, internal memory,
programming, and interfacing capabilities comparable to their
desktop counterparts, while the smaller computers assume that the
buyer/user is willing to forgo some of these features for the
sake of vastly increased portability.

Photos of a standard desktop computer, a suitcase-sized
portable computer, a briefcase computer, and a notebook computer
with captions pointing out the presence or lack of basic system
elements will help illuminate these distinctions.

Rubin/Thinking   10

Portable Peculiarities

Chapter 2 closes with a discussion of buyer and user

considerations about portable computers but not desktop

computers. The section explains that such elements as size,

weight, ruggedness, case integrity, battery life, display

clarity, bundled software, interfaces, and expandability that are

largely peripheral concerns to a desktop-computer buyer are of

far greater importance to somebody shopping for a portable.

Readers are assured that this book, because it concentrates

solely on portables, analyzes these factors thoroughly.

Rubin/Thinking   11

Chapter 3

Do You Need a Portable?   10 pages

The Good News (Or: Why you might)

This section explains the unique virtues of portable
computers such as mobility, ruggedness, price/performance,
bundled software, and compactness. It presents each virtue with
specific examples of why the user might want such a feature.

For example, a person with limited desktop space might want
a portable because it is inherently less bulky than a desktop.
Likewise, a person wishing to have the use of a computer in more
than one place and who lacks the resources to have multiple
computers would welcome the ease of setup and mobility inherent
in a portable.

The person not wishing to agonize over several software
buying decisions might welcome the bundled software most
portables offer, and the person wanting to move the computer
through difficult situations like air or auto travel might like
portable ruggedness as opposed to the relative fragility of
desktop computers.

The Bad News (Or: Why you might not)

This part of the chapter focuses on the drawbacks inherent
in portable computers. The drawbacks may include lack of
expandability, limited display size, limited on-line storage,
smaller keyboards, and lack of numeric keypads. This section
directs readers to take these factors into consideration when

Rubin/Thinking   12

selecting a unit. It examines these drawbacks as they vary from
one category of machine to another, hand-helds vs. full-featured
models.

The chapter closes by posing the rhetorical question: "But
what sorts of things can a portable computer do?" It asks the
reader to turn to the following chapter for the answer.

Rubin/Thinking   13

Chapter 4

Basic Portable Computer Applications   20 pages

The chapter opens by noting that portable computers

basically do what any computer will do. It then defines and

explains the applications for which most people use computers:

word processing, file management, spreadsheets, telecommuni-

cations, programming, and personal productivity.

Along with a definition of each application will be one or

two examples of how the application would fit in in various

business, educational, professional, and personal situations.

The section then suggests readers decide whether there are

one or two primary applications for which they are buying the

computer. It explains that an application will influence the

category and hardware features of the machine considered, and

cautions the buyers that the optimum hardware requirements for

different software packages can vary. For example, word

processing or spreadsheet programs should ideally be used on

equipment with large display and storage capacities, and a

typewriter-style keyboard is a must for word processing.

The chapter and Part I close by saying that users should now

have a good idea of whether or not they need a portable computer

and what they'll do with it if they do, and that they're now

ready to consider their options in the portable computer market,

which follow in Part II.

Rubin/Thinking   14

PART II: THE BUYER'S GUIDE

Chapter 5   25 pages, 2 charts

Four Steps to a Successful Portable Purchase

The chapter begins by introducing this four-step method. It asks readers to follow the steps in order and to complete each step thoroughly before continuing.

Step One: Know What You Want

This step refers readers to a Needs Analysis Chart and asks them to fill it out based on what they think their needs for the computer are likely to be. The chart requests that they list their needs in order of importance, by application, so they can be directed toward a specific group of computers or computer features.

Once they establish their needs, they refer to an Optimum Hardware Configurations Chart. They can look at the configurations for their most important applications and then turn to the hardware guide to look over specific products that match those configurations.

Step Two: Know Your Options

The next step advises readers to look through the hardware guides in Part III based on what they have learned by matching needs with optimum hardware configurations for those needs. It warns that their first and second most important applications may be in conflict with each other in terms of optimum hardware configurations, but they are directed to consider which of the

two applications is more important. This section then urges
readers to use the hardware and software guides to narrow down
their choices of products as much as possible.

Step Three: Find a Source

Once buyers have narrowed the field to a few potential
machines and software products, they should find a source. Step
three then describes possible sources of computers, with their
relative merits and drawbacks. Sources include computer stores,
department stores, mass merchandisers, and mail order. This
section ends by addressing the considerations in making a
purchase: retail vs. discount pricing; availability of service;
after-sale education; selection; expertise of the sales help;
financing; reputation of the vendor; and lack of pressure.

Step Four: Shopping Tips

This step covers these five topics:

1. About advice: from friends, salespeople, other users

2. About retail outlets: good ones and bad ones. . .
    how to tell

3. About salespeople: what you want vs. what they're
    selling, or: beware, "It's just as good as that."

4. About trying machines out: (a) "Being Left Alone,"
    (b) trying to do the work you would be doing,
    (c) personal considerations: feel, look, apparent
        quality, ease of use, ergonomics

5. Getting a discount

Rubin/Thinking   16

    PART III

    Chapter 6

    Suitcase-Sized Portables   75 pages, 24 photos

    This chapter introduces the guide with the explanation that
it has been broken into two chapters, separating the subsets of
portables: suitcase-sized vs. briefcase and notebook computers.
It directs readers to either chapter, since by now their needs
should be well-enough defined so that they know which type of
portable they want.

    The buying guide begins with an examination of the
differences in selection criteria for full-featured computers as
opposed to hand-held models. It describes the criteria for
presentation of full-featured hardware products: price,
operating system, size, weight, display size, keyboard, storage,
RAM size, bundled software, manufacturer's reputation,
documentation, service/warranty, claims to fame, compatibility,
and ruggedness.

    Where software products such as Perfect Writer and Wordstar
are bundled with more than one computer, they are fully evaluated
in the review of the first computer they appear with, and are
discussed under following computers only in relation to any
operating differences they exhibit on that particular machine.

    After this, individual products are presented. Photos of
each product are included. Products presented are Access Matrix,
The Dot, Compaq, PC8086, STAR-lite, Corona Portable PC, Digital

Rubin/Thinking   17

Microsyst DMS-3/F and DMS-15, Dynalogic Hyperion, JONOS Escort

C2100 and C2500, Kaypro II and Kaypro 10, Micro Source M6000P

Voyager, Osborne 1 and Executive, Otrona Attache, Eagle,

Chameleon, SORD Socius M23P, STM Electron PIED PIPER, ZORBA and

NOM1S-9, SKS Nano 2502, TeleVideo TeleTote, Columbia Portable PC,

Commodore Executive 64, Adcock & Johnson Model 3000, and the PMC

MicroMate.

Rubin/Thinking   18

Chapter 7

Briefcase and Notebook Computers   26 pages, 8 photos

This chapter starts by exploring the characteristics
separating briefcase from notebook computers and then lists the
criteria for their evaluations, including battery life/recharge
time, display type and clarity, size, weight, keyboard features,
ROM and RAM size, interfaces, peripherals available, software
available, price, manufacturer's reputation, claims to fame,
documentation, and ruggedness.

The chapter then presents individual products with photos of
each, including the Athena I, the Epson HX-20, the Gavilan, the
Radio Shack Model 100, the Teleram 3000 and 4000, the NEC PC
8200, the Sharp PC-5000, the GRiD Compass.

Rubin/Thinking   19

Chapter 8

Using Your Portable   6 pages, 2 drawings

This chapter offers tips about the care and feeding of a
portable computer:

--user environments: cautions about dust, moisture, etc.

--security: leaving machine unattended in hotels, lockers,
and offices.

--traveling: X-ray checks, airline stowage, power
requirements, backups of disk files, remote service.

Illustrations help clarify sections covering environments
and traveling.

[After the proposal was sold, Charles decided to collaborate on the book
with another writer, Michael McCarthy.]

Bibliography

The Author's Handbook, Franklynn Peterson and Judi Kesselman-Turkel. Englewood Cliffs, N.J.: Prentice-Hall, 1982.

Book Publishing: What It Is, What It Does, 2nd edition, John P. Dessauer. New York: R.R. Bowker Co., 1981.

Books: The Culture and Commerce of Publishing, Lewis A. Coser, Charles Kadushin, and Walter W. Powell. New York: Basic Books, Inc., 1982.

The Complete Guide to Writing Non-Fiction, The American Society of Journalists and Authors, edited by Glen Evans. Cincinnati: Writer's Digest Books, 1983.

The Elements of Style, 3rd edition, William Strunk, Jr. and E.B. White, New York: Macmillan Publishing Co. Inc., 1979

Getting Published: A Guide for Businesspeople and Other Professionals, Gary S. Belkin. New York: John Wiley & Sons, 1984.

How To Be Your Own Literary Agent, Richard Curtis. Boston: Houghton Mifflin Co., 1983.

How to Get Happily Published: A Complete and Candid Guide, Judith Appelbaum and Nancy Evans. New York: New American Library, 1982.

How to Sell What You Write, Jane Adams. New York: G.P. Putnam's Sons, 1984.

How to Write a Winning Proposal, Oscar Collier. New York: American Writer's Corporation, 1982.

How to Write Books that Sell: A Guide to Cashing In on the Booming Book Business, L. Perry Wilbur. Chicago: Contemporary Books, Inc., 1979.

The Literary Agent and the Writer: A Professional Guide, Diane Cleaver. Boston: The Writer, Inc., 1984.

Megatrends: Ten New Directions Transforming Our Lives, John Naisbitt. New York: Warner Books, 1982.

Roget's II: The New Thesaurus by the editors of *The American Heritage Dictionary*. Boston: Houghton Mifflin Co., 1980.

A Writer's Guide to Book Publishing, 2nd edition, Richard Balkin. New York: Hawthorn/Dutton, 1981.

The Writer's Quotation Book: A literary companion, edited by James Charlton. Yonkers: The Pushcart Press, 1980.

The Writer's Survival Manual: The Complete Guide to Getting Your Book Published Right, Carol Meyer. New York: Crown Publishers, Inc., 1982.

Writing and Selling a Nonfiction Book, Max Gunther. Boston: The Writer, Inc., 1973.

Index

About the Author

Michael Larsen worked for three major book publishers before cofounding, in 1972, San Francisco's oldest literary agency—which has since successfully placed hundreds of book proposals and helped hundreds of other authors bring their proposals to professional caliber. In addition to teaching seminars on proposal writing, he and his partner, Elizabeth Pomada, work closely with beginning writers at workshops and conferences throughout the country. Larsen is also the author of the books *California Publicity Outlets* and *Painted Ladies: San Francisco's Resplendent Victorians*; is a founding member of the Independent Literary Agents Association; and has reviewed books for the *San Francisco Chronicle*. Despite his busy schedule, he still finds time to pursue his second love—tap dancing!

More Great Books
For Writers!

Writer's Market—This totally updated edition brings you over 4,000 listings of buyers of freelance work—their names, addresses, submission requirements, contact persons and more! Each listing has been verified for accuracy, 85% have critical information changes over last year and 700 brand new listings have been added! Plus, helpful articles and interviews with top professionals make this your most essential writing resource. #10432/$27.99/1008 pages

The Writer's Ultimate Research Guide—Save research time and frustration with the help of this guide. 352 information-packed pages will point you straight to the information you need to create better, more accurate fiction and nonfiction. With hundreds of listings of books and databases, each entry reveals how current the information is, what the content and organization is like and much more! #10447/$19.99/352 pages

Description—Discover how to use detailed description to awaken the reader's senses, advance the story using only relevant description, create original word depictions of people, animals, places, weather and much more! #10451/$15.99/176 pages

How to Write Like an Expert About Anything—Find out how to use new technology and traditional research methods to get the information you need, envision new markets and write proposals that sell, find and interview experts on any topic and much more! #10449/$17.99/224 pages

How to Write Fast (While Writing Well)—Discover what makes a story and what it takes to research and write one. Then, learn, step-by-step how to cut wasted time and effort by planning interviews for maximum results, beating writer's block with effective plotting, getting the most information from traditional library research and on-line computer bases and much more! Plus, a complete chapter loaded with tricks and tips for faster writing. #10473/$15.99/208 pages/paperback

National Writers Union Guide to Freelance Rates & Standard Practice—A must-have for all freelancers! Tables and charts compiled from surveys of freelance writers, editors and agents give you the going rates for six major freelance markets. Plus, information on rights, the electronic future and more! #10440/$19.95/200 pages/paperback

Writing for Money—Discover where to look for writing opportunities—and how to make them pay off. You'll learn how to write for magazines, newspapers, radio and TV, newsletters, greeting cards and a dozen other hungry markets! #10425/$17.99/256 pages

The Writer's Digest Guide to Manuscript Formats—No matter how good your ideas an unprofessional format will land your manuscript on the slush pile! You need this easy-to-follow guide on manuscript preparation and presentation—for everything from books and articles to poems and plays. #10025/$19.99/200 pages

The Complete Guide to Self Publishing—Discover how to make the publishing industry work for you! You'll get step-by-step guidance on every aspect of publishing from cover design and production tips to sales letters and publicity strategies. #10444/$18.99/432 pages/58 b&w illus/paperback

Magazine Writing That Sells—With this hands-on guide you'll discover how to write the kinds of articles sought and bought by the best magazines. McKinney shows you how to spot great ideas, fire off winning queries and craft evocative, salable articles! *#10409/$16.99/240 pages*

Roget's Superthesaurus—For whenever you need just the right word! You'll find "vocabulary builder" words with pronunciation keys and sample sentences, quotations that double as synonyms, plus the only word-find reverse dictionary in any thesaurus—all in an easy alphabetical format! *#10424/$22.99/624 pages*

Beginning Writer's Answer Book—This book answers 900 of the most often asked questions about the writing process. You'll find business advice, tax tips, plus information about on-line networks, data bases and more. *#10394/$16.99/336 pages*

The Writer's Digest Guide to Good Writing—In one book, you'll find the best in writing instruction gleaned from the past 75 years of *Writer's Digest* magazine! Phenomenally successful authors like Vonnegut, Steinbeck, Oates, Michener and over a dozen others share their secrets on writing technique, idea generation, inspiration and getting published. *#10391/$18.99/352 pages*

Creating Characters—Grab the empathy of your reader with characters so real they'll jump off the page. You'll discover how to make characters come alive with vibrant emotion, quirky personality traits, inspiring heroism, tragic weaknesses and other uniquely human qualities. *#10417/$14.99/192 pages/paperback*

Writing the Blockbuster Novel—Let a top-flight agent show you how to weave the essential elements of a blockbuster into your own novels with memorable characters, exotic settings, clashing conflicts and more! *#10393/$17.99/224 pages*

Writing the Short Story: A Hands-On Program—With Bickham's unique "workshop on paper" you'll plan, organize, write, revise and polish your short story. Clear instruction, helpful charts and practical exercises will lead you every step of the way. *#10421/$16.99/224 pages*

Get That Novel Started! And Keep It Going 'Til You Finish—If you're ready for a no excuses approach to starting and completing your novel, then you're ready for this get-it-going game plan. You'll discover wisdom, experience and advice that helps you latch on to an idea and see it through while avoiding common writing pitfalls. *#10332/$17.95/176 pages*

Thesaurus of Alternatives to Worn-Out Words and Phrases—Rid your work of trite clichés and hollow phrases for good! Alphabetical entries shed light on the incorrect, the bland and the overused words that plague so many writers. Then you'll learn how to vivify your work with alternative, lively and original words! *#10408/$17.99/304 pages*

Voice & Style—Discover how to create character and story voices! You'll learn to write with a spellbinding narrative voice, create original character voices, write dialogue that conveys personality, control tone of voice to create mood and make the story's voices harmonize into a solid style. *#10452/$15.99/176 pages*

Freeing Your Creativity: A Writer's Guide—Discover how to escape the traps that stifle your creativity. You'll tackle techniques for banishing fears and nourishing ideas so you can get your juices flowing again. *#10430/$14.99/176 pages/paperback*

20 Master Plots (And How to Build Them)—Write great contemporary fiction from timeless plots. This guide outlines 20 plots from various genres and illustrates how to adapt them into your own fiction. *#10366/$17.99/240 pages*

Handbook of Short Story Writing, Volume II—Orson Scott Card, Dwight V. Swain, Kit Reed and other noted authors bring you sound advice and timeless techniques for every aspect of the writing process.
#10239/$12.99/252 pages/paperback

How to Write & Sell Your First Novel—Improve your chances for getting your first (or any) novel published by learning the successful strategies of other first time writers. You also get do's and don'ts on editorial submission, marketing advice and news on the latest, best-selling genres. *#10168/$13.99/230 pages/paperback*

Make Your Words Work—Loaded with samples and laced with exercises, this guide will help you clean up your prose, refine your style, strengthen your descriptive powers, bring music to your words and much more!
#10399/$14.95/304 pages/paperback

The 29 Most Common Writing Mistakes And How to Avoid Them—Weak comparisons, too many adjectives, excessive self-expression—with clarity and good humor, Delton shows how to correct these and 26 other common writing mistakes to help you get published! *#10221/$9.95/96 pages/paperback*

Writing the Novel: From Plot to Print—Block, author of more than 100 published novels, answers the questions that plague both novice and experienced novelists and leads you step-by-step toward getting published.
#02747/$11.95/218 pages/paperback

The Complete Guide to Writing Fiction—This concise guide will help you develop the skills you need to write and sell long and short fiction. You'll get a complete rundown on outlining, narrative writing details, description, pacing and action. *#10158/$18.95/312 pages*